AF865311

Decline and Falling Over

Decline and Falling Over

JO BRAND

MICHAEL PENGUIN Est. 1935 JOSEPH

PENGUIN MICHAEL JOSEPH

UK | USA | Canada | Ireland | Australia
India | New Zealand | South Africa

Penguin Michael Joseph is part of the Penguin Random House group of companies whose addresses can be found at global.penguinrandomhouse.com

Penguin Random House UK,
One Embassy Gardens, 8 Viaduct Gardens, London SW11 7BW

penguin.co.uk

First published 2026
001

Copyright © Jo Brand, 2026

The moral right of the author has been asserted

Penguin Random House values and supports copyright. Copyright fuels creativity, encourages diverse voices, promotes freedom of expression and supports a vibrant culture. Thank you for purchasing an authorized edition of this book and for respecting intellectual property laws by not reproducing, scanning or distributing any part of it by any means without permission. You are supporting authors and enabling Penguin Random House to continue to publish books for everyone. No part of this book may be used or reproduced in any manner for the purpose of training artificial intelligence technologies or systems. In accordance with Article 4(3) of the DSM Directive 2019/790, Penguin Random House expressly reserves this work from the text and data mining exception

Set in 14.8/18pt Garamond Premier Pro
Typeset by Six Red Marbles UK, Thetford, Norfolk
Printed and bound in Great Britain by Clays Ltd, Elcograf S.p.A.

The authorized representative in the EEA is Penguin Random House Ireland, Morrison Chambers, 32 Nassau Street, Dublin D02 YH68

A CIP catalogue record for this book is available from the British Library

HARDBACK ISBN: 978–0–241–82219–7

Penguin Random House is committed to a sustainable future for our business, our readers and our planet. This book is made from Forest Stewardship Council® certified paper. For more information on our environmental initiatives please visit penguin.co.uk

MIX
Paper
FSC® C018179

To all the people getting older who don't want to grow up.

Contents

INTRODUCTION

As someone who is, quite frankly, relatively immature, I do find it hard to accept that I am being gradually propelled towards the top of the hill and will soon be over it.

Among things like friends, foods I shouldn't eat and laughs, I love words – and for old age there are plenty. I am nearer to my *dotage*, a state of *senescence*, *decrepitude*, *antiquity*, or admission to Batty Old Lady Land than most (even those older than me), and, depending on your viewpoint, on the cusp of entering 'the golden years' or 'the winter of my life'. I am hoping for golden with the odd cold snap, but who knows? Will I be a rheumy-eyed, contented matriarch nodding by the fire, surrounded by a loving, attentive family, or will I be a swivel-eyed, ancient, portly she-wolf refusing to go 'gentle into that good night' and pissing everyone right off? Well, the second one sounds a lot more fun, doesn't it, and I suspect the more likely. And if I'm not having many lols along the way, I certainly hope I can, at least, unwittingly provide some you'll-never-guess-what-she's-gone-and-done-now type laughs for my family and friends.

Much as I want to present you with a shining vision of my divine future and tell you how wonderful old age can be, I feel like I can't venture down that route wholeheartedly because life is not like that for most people as things stand. So I suppose this is an attempt to collect all the bits of my past and present together and weave them into a realistic portrait of old age. And because I am an incorrigible cynic, it will inevitably be a slightly jaded vision of the future, though hopefully one with plenty of laughs along the way. People often say when faced with the messy business of life, 'I didn't know whether to laugh or cry.' I do, and it's laugh. Not one of us knows what is going to happen next week, let alone in that shrinking distant future. And hallelujah to that. Who wants to look into a crystal ball and see a perfectly accurate future? Not me, guv, and I suspect it's the same for pretty much everyone else.

So how will I go about this business of ageing? Where do you go and what do you do when you're getting old? How can you best organize your shitter second half? Well, that's a very big question with no right answer, but stay tuned for a bungled assortment of musings. I should point out that it's very unlikely I will be offering wise words. As the well-known philosopher Jimi Hendrix said, 'Knowledge speaks, but wisdom listens,' and I am a really terrible listener. And anyway, I prefer Oscar Wilde's 'Life is too important to be taken seriously.' I suppose what I'm trying to say is that this is not a particularly sober book, though I doubt that you were expecting a learned treatise on growing old gracefully because if there's one thing I've never been, it's graceful.

Human beings are an endless variety of weird and wonderful, so attempting to encapsulate the many ways people skip, limp, shuffle, sky-dive or prance into their older years would be impossible in these pages, but I would hope you might get the following:

A laugh
Some entertainment
Some interesting, quirky information
More of a what-not-to-do list

So please sit back, relax and enjoy this completely unscientific, largely unresearched set of opinions based on my age and very particular life experiences, and my, at times, fruitless attempts to pull them together into a coherent order. At least we've all got one thing in common: we're all getting older.

CHAPTER ONE

Fossilized Influencers

Hello, I am an officially designated 'old person' according to the World Health Organization, which I find surprising, as my idea of 'old' involves a walking stick and a bun. (Not the edible sort.) But being old has crept up on me like an over-enthusiastic chugger and as I presume most people do, I look in the mirror and don't think I look that old. However, compared to many of my peers I look like a recently slept-in bed.

What is 'old' and what does 'old' look like to you? Grey hair? Wrinkles? No discernible ankles? It's impossible to try and find a meaning that applies to everyone apart from chronological age, so we might as well stop trying. Old age is both subjective and objective. Yes, in the past, most old women used to have grey hair, but now there's a choice. Some women have wrinkles, some don't. Some smell of old age, some don't. What does ageing even smell like? Mustiness? Lavender? A faint whiff of urine?

(I'm always tempted to say the latter when someone asks me which perfume I've got on, but then again, I have a terrible and inappropriate sense of humour which often gets me into trouble.)

Depending on what age you are, you will have a very specific picture in your mind of what old age looks like which relies on so many variables, including your own family, prevailing ideas about appearance, and the general attitudes towards age in your own culture.

My earliest idea of what old age looks like comes from the late 1950s and early 1960s, because I was just getting to the age when I was becoming more aware of my surroundings and the sort of people that populated them. At the age of 5, anyone over the age of 25 looked like an old person to me, so I was not a great judge of chronological age. It seemed to me at the time that most women wore tailored, full-skirted, flowery dresses. The horror! (I am genetically incapable of wearing anything smart or expensive and keeping it looking good for any longer than about twenty minutes.) Also, most women had some sort of perm, whether they were 25 or 50. I cherish a picture of my mum with her friends when she was 18 years old in the 1950s and, quite honestly, they could all have passed for 35, so conservative do they look. They also seemed to be adhering to a uniform code of 'Everyone must look like a shrub'. A similar group picture of me and my friends at the same age could not have been more different. Scruffy, comfortable, shoeless, we looked like we were about to be arrested by the fashion police, a source of shame to our parents who despaired at our apparent lack of self-care and self-respect.

In the 1960s a fashion earthquake happened, because women were becoming freer and not expected to adhere to the general rules of conformity. Overnight, dresses became much shorter, miniskirts happened and everything was brightly coloured with geometrical shapes and worn with many a shiny PVC cap. My mum missed out on this look by a good few years (thankfully, as she would have looked so disturbing). She continued to dress quite conservatively whilst women fifteen years younger went for it big-time. Teenagers hadn't been invented during my mother's adolescence, so she belonged to the last generation of women who could have passed as their mothers.

As time moves on, and given the plethora of what I will call 'disguises' for ageing, things have changed quite radically. Choice is rife, from slapping on a bit of cream to smooth out future wrinkles now, to lying unconscious under a surgeon's knife, with your fingers crossed, and seeing what your new 'young' face looks like when you wake up, all the way through to a jam and mongoose sperm emulsion. All right, I made that one up. Suffice to say, surgical procedures have improved, thankfully, as some poor women in the past have woken up looking like nothing they had imagined.

Let's talk wrinkles! These seem to be the major indicator of the ageing process and a phenomenon many women have felt inclined to tackle. Me, not so much. And, of course, if you are thinnish – which is, let's face it, alas the socially preferred presentation for most women – you will look wrinkly more quickly, so my advice would be to put a bit of weight on: fill your face to fill out your face. One option for surgeons is to take some fat from somewhere else on your body and transfer it to underneath the wrinkly bits on your face, so with my weight-gain method you will be saving time and avoid the very inconvenient intervention of fat transfer. Sorry, this is a bit tongue-in-cheek, but that was never a good way to pad out your wrinkles, in my book. I will try to take it more seriously.

The other issue is that it's difficult to avoid prevailing fashion in terms of appearance – for example, bums became more filled out for a bit but are now being shunned for a more natural approach. 'Big arse bad' to 'big arse good' and back again in such a short time!

The problem with becoming old is that to the outside world, people, especially women, have a tendency to lose their definition. They become clichéd anonymous blobs who all look the same to younger people, except, weirdly, we anonymous blobs still look the same to our friends and family as we did when we were younger. If you see pictures of older people in times gone by (let's face it, mainly women) in domestic settings, to be quite honest it would be hard, sometimes, to pick one of them out of a line-up (and let me say I am in favour of criminal gangs made up of old women).

This has certainly changed in the six or so decades since I was a child, as options are now on offer to do things like stretch your skin so tight across your face, smiling is virtually an Olympic sport. Along with this, women are presented with a dizzying array of creams, procedures and random advice to 'youthanize' themselves to within an inch of their lives, as the hitherto skin-smoothing business has now become global and the world menu of what's on offer, pricewise, varies so wildly it is tempting for some of us to venture into less regulated climes to get a much cheaper deal as it can be prohibitively expensive here. Tummy-tuck-versus-house-extension territory. These trips are always in good faith and on the whole men and women come back happy.

The truth of ageing is that some people don't care about the changes in their appearance as they age and other people care a lot. Women always used to care much more than men, but men are now catching up. Treatments for men which were unheard of when I was younger are now embraced. In the bad old days, men would just comb their hair and turn their pants inside out and they were done for the week. I don't care that much and never really have done about hanging on to a youthful appearance. On the other hand, I do get my hair dyed so I must care a bit. It's because letting it grow out makes me look like a badger.

As we grow up, we all build an image of what ageing means based on the older people we know. Several women have influenced my attitude towards old age in all its various incarnations. Some of these women, I feel, are absolutely admirable, whereas others made me think, 'I hope I'm not like that when I'm old.' Let me introduce you to my early role models.

Mrs M

The first old person I really became aware of outside my immediate family was 'Mrs M' and I suppose I first noticed her when I was about four years old. Bear that in mind, as my reaction to her was purely based on the comparison with my relatives and the fear of wicked witches from various stories that had been read to me.

She lived in the basement flat below our house in London, and we very rarely saw her out and about. She had the old woman's uniform at the time of white hair and a shapeless dress, which was further hidden by the pinny/tabard combination, which is much beloved of dinner ladies. And whilst we're on the subject, can I just put in a good word for dinner ladies, who have always been the butt of jokes over the years and portrayed as a combination of frumpy, grumpy and lumpy. What's wrong with that? These are my major aims for old age, and they are my role models. No one ever looked at miners or binmen and thought, 'Look at the state of them, no effort whatsoever!' To me their relentless pursuit of the practical, the protective, and not giving a shit what people thought of them was a badge of honour. As you can tell, I am in favour of older women sticking two fingers up at others' expectations.

Mrs M had some grim slippers and looked angry most of the time and I was scared of her. We avoided her mostly, until one day, whilst playing outside her flat, that all changed. She appeared at the door, remarked that it was very hot and we must be thirsty and invited us in for a drink. I don't think any of us wanted to, but unfortunately, my mum had drummed into us that we must be polite. So in we trooped and were met with the sight of the most neglected and (sorry, Mrs M) filthy kitchen I had ever seen. Given I was four years old, that wasn't a difficult ambition to achieve. On top of a sticky table covered with crumbs, a dish of highly aromatic ancient old cat food and a spread of barely recognizable household detritus, stood a half-full blue bottle of sterilized milk which had been colonized by huge flies (bluebottles, ironically).

I was aghast in a four-year-old kind of way as my

brothers and I stood rooted to the spot while Mrs M collected three grubby chipped teacups from the draining board and sloshed a generous amount of the milk into each one. This was called 'sterilized milk' in the olden days and it was treated by being heated to a very high temperature to kill all the microorganisms and therefore you didn't need to refrigerate it. So you could leave it out for days and give the flies a party, and no one, in my opinion, would drink it unless they had a gun to their head. It tasted *revolting*.

Again, continuing down the route of politeness, we all felt obliged at the very least to make a show of having some of the milk. I took a small gulp and just the act of doing so made me feel like I was going to throw up. I noticed my brothers were edging towards the door. I took another big gulp, swallowed it and managed to call 'Thanks' as I headed towards the door. Somewhere between Mrs M's flat and our bathroom I projectile vomited, but thankfully Mrs M never saw it and, as far as I can remember, we never really saw her again. I seem to recall my mum saying something like, 'Well done, I know none of you wanted to go.' I think I had a very early experience of the proverb, 'No good deed ever goes unpunished'. Looking back on it, I realize I was a very judgemental four-year-old, but at least I didn't express any of that out loud to Mrs M. To meet a woman like her was terrifying, put me off sterilized milk for life and presented me with a totally different lifestyle, which I just didn't understand at the time, although I do think now that she was probably struggling and in retrospect, she was just trying to be nice and neighbourly.

Mrs and Miss F

The next older women I met who had an impact on me were completely different. We had moved out of London to a small village in Kent where we lived in a house next door to a huge flamboyant manor house. Our neighbours were a woman, probably in her late fifties, and her mother, who I imagine was in her late seventies or early eighties. These two were a complete contrast to Mrs M, our previous scary, ankle-less neighbour, and they were very, very posh. This was my welcome to the world of very wealthy people and it was hard to believe that only two of them occupied a house ten times the size of ours. Whereas Mrs M had been a bit 'gor blimey guv'nor', these two had cut-glass accents – the old Mrs F pronounced 'donkey' as 'dunkey', which we all thought was hilarious.

Everything about them bellowed money. The house was huge with large grounds and was stuffed full of opulent furniture, oil paintings and expensive kitchenware, not to mention the manicured gardens which seemed to stretch a very long way. As I was probably about eight years old at the time I was very impressed by them, although I think I probably began to feel the stirrings of a left-wing commitment coming down the line.

Both of them were imperious in their own way. Miss F was enormously glamorous: in fact, it made me wonder why she hadn't been snapped up by 'Lord-Someone-or-Other'. She wore big sunglasses all day and a Princess Anne headscarf, rode horses and swept into rooms like a duchess. Looking back, she was probably the same age as Mrs M from Clapham, but she couldn't have been more different: a stylish, slim, slacks-wearer with identifiable ankles. Her mother was equally horsey in nature, if not a rider, was always swathed in expensive clothes and used a stick. She had her hair in the obligatory perm of the day and I'm sure I made a mental note to never have a perm right then and there. Miss F hee-hawed sentences at us while Mrs F barked them. They made us a rather hideous meal one day, when the staff were off (one very quiet Spanish woman who glided silently around the house, and a gardener). Normally I love cheese on toast, but this tasted horrible – thankfully, it was a quarter of the size of what we were used to, so not difficult to finish.

Their house seemed to us to be from another era and Mrs F told us that it was haunted by a ghost called Kitty Fisher, immortalized in the nursery rhyme 'Lucy Locket

Lost Her Pocket'. Kitty Fisher, incidentally, was a courtesan who had married the Lord of Another Manor Just Down the Road – that manor being a huge stately home which eventually became Benenden School for girls.

One day, the two women invited my brothers and me to stay the night in their house in the hope we might see the ghost, as we had very rudely asked if we could, without telling our mum. It all went slightly awry. I woke in the night, fell out of bed, ran into the hall, spotted an over-lit ghostly portrait of a woman on the wall and, in my half-awake state, thought it was *the* ghost so ran downstairs and across the garden, squealing, and banged on our front door until my mum let me in. My brothers slept peacefully through the night and wandered home in the morning.

I suppose the difference between these two women and all the other people I had come across in life up to that point gave me a future clue to the contrasting lives of people and the ever more yawning gap as they aged. We all preferred the older Mrs F. She seemed a bit lonely and was much chattier, whereas her daughter had the distance that wealthy people tend to put between themselves and the plebs. Maybe I'm being unfair; she was perfectly nice to us, but the older woman was kind and that's always been at the top of my list.

Betsey Trotwood

When I was at primary school in a small village in Kent, most of the kids in my class thought I was odd because we discussed politics at home and, the horror, read books. My mum and dad had met through the Young Socialists, talked about politics all the time and encouraged us to read 'proper books'. This of course immediately excluded me from any hope of ever being a 'popular girl', but led me to meet many literary heroines, including my role model for not ageing gracefully at all: Betsey Trotwood from *David Copperfield*.

As a 12-year-old (me, not her), Betsey was one of my heroines. Yes, we didn't have social media and were not allowed to watch TV in the daytime. Deprived or what? Had I had the opportunity to scroll through a phone at that time I probably would have done, but it was books, radio or nothing, and on the rare occasions when neither of my parents were in, my brothers and I always took the opportunity to watch some crappy TV and wash our brains in educationally pointless but delicious soaps, which my mum massively disapproved of. She had some very strict rules. We weren't really allowed to watch commercial channels because she hated adverts and the relentless twaddle used to sell products to people. To this day I'm afraid I still can't bring myself to watch them and, irritatingly, to wind people up, I constantly quote George Orwell's cutting words that ads are 'the rattling of a stick inside a swill bucket'. (If you think I'm being a bit preachy here, I am.) Consequently, I ended up reading a fair bit of Dickens as a kid and although, I grant you, there are lots of long, torturous passages that made me want to tear my hair out and read *Jackie* magazine (except I wasn't allowed to), they are great stories.

What I loved about Betsey was that she had a personality. I bet she could have done a brilliant podcast about being old. (Incidentally, I have considered doing a podcast about getting old, but I have the old person's disease of 'can't-be-arsedness'.) I admit I found many Dickens women somewhat anodyne and a bit wet. Yes, they were pretty and sweet, but the ones who were either disturbed, angry, unpleasant or just plain nasty were always much more interesting than the droopy helpless ones. In many Victorian novels you tend to have a 'fallen woman' who is shunned by society for allowing a man to 'have his way with her'. I always wanted to be a 'fallen woman' and perhaps now I will be, but not in the interesting sense of the word. No blame ever fell on the man himself, of course, as he happily worked his way through a slew of women, emerging with his reputation intact. That unsatisfactory situation has not been quite so easy as of late.

Betsey is tough, funny, independent and in charge

of her own destiny. Also, Dickens shows us that despite the somewhat brittle and bad-tempered exterior, Betsey Trotwood has the proverbial heart of gold. However, if you're thinking, 'God, she sounds annoying,' maybe you should read someone else's old lady book.

Betsey Trotwood is an early incarnation of what I imagine was an older grumpy Suffragette. Her pedigree for this involves having been abandoned by a pretty useless and unpalatable husband and, as she is an independent woman who (lucky for her) can support herself, she doesn't need to rely on potential crumbs thrown in her direction. Of course no one used the 'feminist' word in those days, as neither the word nor the concept had even occurred to anyone, because at that time women belonged to their husbands, had to do as they were told and just silently seethe. However, despite her being tough and uncompromising, Betsey is actually a very kind person, who hides it very well indeed by shouting quite a lot and running around waving a big stick. It's good to keep people on their toes by being grumpy, I think. I plan to increase my grumpiness by about 5–10 per cent a year, so if I get to 80, I will be unbearable and rather than having to ask my family to care for me, they'll be quite happy to take the initiative and push me out of a moving car.

Betsey Trotwood, David's great-aunt, is very pissed off when David turns out not to be the niece she hoped for.

However, she becomes one of his greatest supporters in the end, which I think is very generous of her. The same goes for a man called Mr Dick – not her personal choice of name, but a man who I suspect these days would be on the autistic spectrum. Betsey rescues Mr Dick from an asylum where he is incarcerated and he comes to live with her in her house where she takes care of him. To me, this is a real sign of commitment, and I can't think of many people that would be prepared to take this on.

Betsey Trotwood and I part ways on one of her major issues in *David Copperfield* and that is donkeys. Donkeys constantly graze on Betsey's very well-kept lawn and it drives her insane, but it is this part of the story that introduces a comedy element to Betsey as she runs out with her maid Janet and a big stick, threatening injury to the boys who are looking after the donkeys as they chomp on the front lawn. (The donkeys not the boys.)

I think personality looms big with Betsey Trotwood and although I'm in no way saying that many of us kind of forget older people have a personality, society does tend to forget this . . . just like I do with the men I think of as deserving of the name 'Mr Dick'.

A Weird and Scary Day Out

When I was a student nurse in the late 1970s, I worked on a mental health ward for the elderly, and part of the job was occasionally spending the day with someone in their home to assess how well they would cope if they were discharged from hospital care. I was asked to spend most of the day with a woman who was in her late seventies and suffering from an illness which involved considerable paranoia on her part. We were dropped off at her flat on a large estate (council, not country) in south London at about 10 a.m. The minibus driver, a lovely guy in his thirties, waved a cheery goodbye and headed off, having said he'd be back about 4 p.m.

Almost as soon as we got inside her flat the atmosphere changed. The woman began to pile furniture up against the door in the fashion of a barricade. My somewhat pathetic entreaties fell on deaf ears and so I waited until she took a breath and said, 'We don't really need all this up against the door,' and began to slide away two chairs which had been upended and pushed against a pile of other random bits of furniture. What happened next really took me by surprise. She whacked me extremely hard on the arm and, God, it *really* hurt. This dispelled another one of my delusions that a 70-year-old woman was not very good at punching.

I had to reassess the situation very quickly and had visions of me on the floor, unconscious after a few rounds. So, with a view to maintaining as much peaceful interaction as possible, I decided not to try to dismantle her handiwork again and I kept my distance. Of course this was the era of no mobile phones, so I had no choice but to wait until 4 p.m., praying that the friendly minibus driver would be back on time. I did think about shouting 'Help!' out of the window but wasn't sure anyone would have time to rescue me before I was battered to a pulp. So I trod carefully around her for about six hours until the driver knocked at the door. The relief! I'd been instructed that I was not allowed to let anyone in, but managed to relay this message to him very quickly before receiving a smack round the back of the head.

I'm not sure how the message was communicated, but it was decided that the driver would get in through the window while I distracted my charge. Thank God he was quick. I remember thinking, 'Now he's going to get some of what I had.' But no – as soon as he appeared, he was welcomed like a long-lost relative, managing, I have to say, to make me look like a complete amateur (which I was).

My beliefs about older women all being weak and defenceless took a bit of a hit that day. (Sorry.) In some ways it's reassuring. In the vernacular of the time, she was 'built like a brick shithouse', and despite being on the receiving end, I rather admired her. I'm not a fan of violence in any form, but looking back and thinking about the times my dad lost his temper and lashed out at me, her right hook would have come in very handy.

Tante Dinne

Or 'Auntie Dinne', as she was known, was the elderly German aunt of my younger brother Matt's wife Bibi, and shared a home with Bibi's parents. I met her when we went out to Germany for Matt's wedding. Whilst I was out there, I don't really remember Tante Dinne ever moving from her position by the kitchen table. I would guess she was in her late eighties. Her main occupations seemed to be peeling vegetables, drinking coffee, smiling and nodding. It seemed idyllic to me at the time, although it was only a brief snapshot and I mention her because she was part of the family furniture and was cared for by them.

What Tante Dinne represents to me is the appealing concept of incorporating a much older person into your family who is loved, content and doing as much as she can do without any pressure. Then again, in the future, would I want to sit in the family kitchen peeling vegetables? Nope.

My Mum

The final older woman who left a very strong impression on me and was magnificent in so many ways was, of course, my mum. She was a complex individual, but I loved the fact that she just wasn't like other people's mums. I didn't really notice this until I was a bit older.

As I have mentioned, when I was a child, I thought my mum was very, very old. I can remember when I was about five, thinking that she was probably about 50, when in fact she was only 27. And then when she actually *was* old, she didn't seem old at all.

Five-year-olds think everyone over the age of 12 is old as they don't know very much and anyone who isn't wearing a bib any more is edging that way.

Grown-ups in the 1950s, judged by today's standards, dressed in quite a conservative fashion and all looked very similar in their old-lady clothes and stockings/tights, which made their legs look slightly weird, an unsavoury muddy colour a lot of them. These were normally accompanied by high-heeled shoes – just not your Christian Louboutins or your Jimmy Choos, because they, fashioned by men, are more about aesthetics than practicality, tottering about with your womb tilted (a serious fact I was informed of at school). What did I care at the time if my womb was tilted? I barely knew where it was, what it did and often wondered in the Christmas carol why God abhorred not the one that belonged to the Virgin Mary. (It's always good not to abhor wombs, in my book.) No, ladies' day-to-day shoes were not built for hooking a husband in those days, though, to some extent, hooking a husband *was* very important back then as a man *completed* you like you were a jigsaw. It was the other way round, given the amount of running around women had to do. Fifties ladies' shoes were sort of ugly, sort of chunky, thoroughly uninspiring and often accompanied by an apron.

Do women still wear aprons? My mum certainly did and as you got older, aprons morphed from something pretty and tied at the waist – as if you only chucked gravy over your lower portions – into the full-body tabard thing, plain-ish and rather drab sometimes, to designate you were at the *next stage* of your life, your womb had had it, and it didn't really matter that you looked like a sack of potatoes.

My mum never really moved on to the tabard stage as her homely lady pursuits had been replaced by an ambition to become a social worker (cue sympathy or disdain).

Women had very similar hairstyles in the fifties too. Nothing spiky, nothing pink and mainly curled in a very similar fashion to that which you will spot on much older women today.

And most women looked like clones of each other. As

I mentioned before, the picture of my mum and friends identically dressed became a different picture as women freed themselves from the shackles of male expectations. Well, some of them did, and they included my mum . . . eventually.

As my mum aged, she did develop an individual taste in clothes, which accompanied her all the way through to the end of her life. I hate to say this, but her clothes were not to my taste; nor mine to hers, come to that. After the flowery-dress stage that I remember as a child, my mum's taste in clothes veered much more towards the practical, but still in a womanly kind of way. So, for example, I never ever saw her wearing trousers, not even a rogue pair of 'slacks', as they tended to be called in those days. For my mum it was skirts and jumpers mainly, with fairly sensible comfortable shoes, something I would not dream of wearing. I can honestly say that in all the pictures of my mum that I have (a lot), there isn't a single one in which she is wearing anything I liked. This is probably more of a reflection of my taste rather than hers. She had a chain belt at some point, for God's sake. Why???? I'm not saying any of her clothes were awful, I just didn't like them. I think there was something of the 'lady' about them, and those sorts of clothes are about as far away from what I wanted to wear as you could get. There's a picture of my grandma Maisie, my mum and me at my aunt's wedding when I was in my early twenties, and fair play to us, we all looked absolutely *appalling.* Both my mum and Grandma Maisie were in pastel-coloured dresses with hideous hats, and I had on some sort of light-pink patterned jumpsuit. The horror! It was as if I'd become detached from reality in some way. I've never worn pink since. I also once caught my mum wearing a crocheted poncho and on another occasion a sort of jerkin thing.

My mum definitely felt similarly about what I wore. She would occasionally ask me, 'Are you wearing that tonight?' in a slightly strained way, as if I had Lady Gaga's meat dress on. I also remember how relieved I was when I could buy my own clothes as, hideous as they may have been to my mum, it was a relief to stop wearing someone else's choices. I don't know why I have such a visceral reaction to clothes I don't like. Must ask a therapist sometime. So, I think we just quietly agreed to disagree about each other's choices in most areas and sartorial peace was maintained.

It's quite hard to pinpoint when my mum started to seem old. I noticed it most when I hadn't seen her for a while. My mum is from the Never-Say-Anything-About-Your-Health generation and pumping her for information was like getting blood out of the proverbial stone, whereas my dad would happily describe everything that was happening with him in intricate precision. My mum, however, kept even the smallest details to herself. There were occasional clues that things were wrong when I was a child because I would very occasionally hear her sounding as if she might be in pain, but she completely denied it and, to be honest, a professional interrogator wouldn't have fared any better. I could understand it when I was young, but as an adult she was exactly the same.

When my mum moved to Ludlow from London in the late 1980s, this created a big geographical gulf which meant I didn't see her nearly as often and so was unable to even assess visually what was going on with her. In her sixties, she had a heart attack but chose not to tell me or my brothers at the time and left it a couple of weeks until after she was out of hospital. I was fairly appalled she hadn't told me as soon as it happened. That very much set the pattern for the future, and she was pretty guarded about her health after that. I rushed up to visit as soon as she told me what was going on and stayed for a few days. It turned out she hadn't gone straight to hospital when she had chest pain, because she didn't think it was that bad and, unfortunately, when she did finally relent, it turned out she had done some permanent damage to her heart. Whether it would have made any difference if I had been there, I doubt.

One day I went out to do some shopping and arrived back to find her lying on her front beside the television. I panicked, thinking she'd had another heart attack, and I think I managed an agonized squawk, at which point she turned her face towards me and said, 'I'm trying to programme the video, it's driving me mad.'

I did say to her while I was there that she must let me know if there was anything going on with her health, but she didn't, and so it proved an ongoing battle to attempt to find out any details at all until things had reached a crisis of some sort. A mixture of stubbornness, not wanting to worry my brothers and me, and just her nature meant self-sufficiency taken to the absolute maximum. I'm not sure how you get round this problem with a parent. I had to rely on her friends. She drove me mad but I think one of the most impressive things about my mum was her fearlessness. She graffitied buildings, interrupted council meetings and generally made a nuisance of herself when she felt any infringement of decency had occurred. And I couldn't ask for a better mum than that.

HOW YOU KNOW YOU'RE GETTING ON: A CHECKLIST

You may achieve the following in a slightly different order or not at all, but tick the box when you recognize you've started down this route.

- ☐ You tut at a new word a 'young person' uses.
- ☐ You watch half an episode of a series on catch-up before it occurs to you you've already seen it.
- ☐ You call your husband/partner 'Malcolm' for no reason whatsoever.
- ☐ You throw an ancient frying pan away because you can't be bothered to wash it up.
- ☐ You find a screwdriver in your handbag.
- ☐ You sleep on an armchair because you can't be arsed to go to bed.
- ☐ You can't think of the word for blancmange.
- ☐ You don't change a lightbulb because you can't be bothered to get a ladder out or risk balancing on a wobbly chair.

- ☐ You take the wrong bag to a charity shop.
- ☐ You can't remember why you've got an onion in your hand.
- ☐ You call your cat in when you haven't got a cat.
- ☐ You get in the shower with your slippers on.

CHAPTER TWO

How the Human Crumbles

The more you age, the more rubbish stuff is advancing inside your body that you can't see. Lots of people will escape completely unscathed as they pass through the portals of 70 and 80, but for the lucky ones like me it's started a bit earlier.

Obviously what's going on outside your body is visible to the eye, but it's what's going on inside that is a mystery and not an exciting one. Current circumstances dictate that if there is a reason you feel you need to have some sort of scan, you'll have to wait until there is more evidence for it rather than just an ache or a pain, because those pleas to the doctor that you're sure there's something wrong simply aren't enough to get the ball rolling.

I would imagine that as technology ramps up to the max, surely it won't be that long before we're able to see inside our bodies with a little hand-held scanner we can buy online, giving us a more accurate picture of how long we're going to last, what needs doing and when.

Imagine strolling in the park with a friend – wouldn't it be lovely to sit on a bench comparing vital organs, rather than just speculating about what could be going on with pain number 3 or pain number 7? Of course, the legend is that older people spend a lot of time rambling on about their aches and pains. Yes, I do this, but not to people on the train or at family weddings. No, it's much more appropriate if you have that special friend who can match you ache for pain as you detail your lists to each other and have a bloody good laugh while you're doing it.

As we plummet towards old age our genetic programming starts to kick in, and you realize why, for example, your hands look weird. Arthritis: thank you, Grandma! I've used the word *plummet*, but I know some people glide effortlessly towards old age, it's just that I'm not one of them and I'm the one writing this book.

All the people who put in the hard work keeping fit, eating healthily, not smoking and not lying face down drunk in a gutter, apart from being very annoying will feel the benefit of their dedication. Well, hopefully they will. Imagine putting in all that work and it not adding a few more years on – you'd be raging. I say this from the standpoint of somebody whose half-hearted attempts at maintaining any consistency in terms of life-enhancing changes have been absolutely bloody useless. Quite a lot of humanity has the new-year's-resolution approach to health, and many of us a tendency not to even make it to the end of January.

But the feeling that your body is beginning to let you down is relative. For example, not being able to run 200 metres in under five minutes is not going to worry me ever, whereas if you are the world-record holder for that distance, it's quite a different kettle of fish. Bodily decline is a completely subjective judgement depending on your starting point. Every experience we have is a spectrum along which is strung every kind of ability, so let's just have a run, jog, trot, stagger or crawl through them, depending on where you're at.

Sight

The vast majority of people will experience deteriorating eyesight as they age, but most of them will be able to see stuff with varying strengths of contact lenses or glasses. Apparently 80 per cent of information we get is acquired through sight, which makes Seeing Stuff the queen of the senses, and most of us will experience our vision becoming less efficient, but not failing altogether.

Driving is a good example. I used to drive myself everywhere, any distance at any time of day or night, no matter how exhausted I was. These days I sometimes feel like a batty old aunt in a Morris Minor narrowly avoiding clipping obstacles. I do know, though, that this sort of mental state can strike at other times in one's life. 'Baby brain', one of the many kinds of mental fog experienced by women, seems to be a very well-established phenomenon, as attested to by someone I knew who drove off with their baby secured in their car seat, the only issue being the car seat was on the roof of the car. Thankfully they realized in time. (It wasn't me!)

And baby brain returns some years later disguised as extremely mature brain, but our eyes have aged along with us and apparently can't handle these *modern* LED and HID/xenon headlights on other cars. Our poor old dim eyes just get dazzled. Apparently, this issue is not going to be solved quickly in any meaningful way, so you may have to attempt stretches of the motorway with your eyes shut to minimize the glare. Good luck, everyone.

Also, I am more rubbish at parking than I used to be, and it has been remarked on more than once that my passenger might need a lift to the kerb. The solution to this is not giving anyone a lift, least of all a baby.

I do, like many people, wear glasses, which I think are very useful compared to contact lenses, which never really worked for me. Fine putting them in, but having to do a pinching action anywhere near your eyeball to remove them is a very serious mistake for a champion mega-fumbler like me. I tried a couple of times, pinched my actual eyeball and gave up. When you're older, how are you going to manage that when you can't see a bloody thing anyway?

However, glasses not only restore to you the gift of sight, but protect your eyes against misadventure. Without them, you may be walking through some woods and get a sharp twig right in the iris, or examine a pan of hot oil rather too closely or, most likely, poke yourself in the eye with a pen or similar. I've also found the style of glasses I wear to be very useful for disguising very sparse eyebrows. My poor eyebrows all but disappeared in the 1970s because it was fashionable to pluck them into a single arched line of individual hairs. The year 1971 saw me lay waste to my virtual monobrow and Groucho Marx thickness. When my mum saw them, she was *furious*. They did look awful, if I'm honest. She said they would never grow back, but I scoffed at that statement and, of course, she turned out to be right. In 2022 one of my daughters sported those very same Groucho Marx eyebrows which were very on point – or whatever the current expression is – while the top of my poor ageing face shivered away with minimal cover. My glasses somehow manage to disguise the bags under my eyes very well too, as the rim at the bottom slightly follows their line and it saves having to go under the surgeon's knife.

Hearing

I don't hear a lot of what people say. That's 80 per cent down to me not listening. Hearing loss is common as we get older; about a third of people over the age of 60 experience it. My smartwatch tells me if I'm in an environment that is too loud and advises me to take evasive action. And I admit that on several occasions I have used earplugs, particularly when my husband is talking about rugby, not to mention at a couple of events where the singer is screaming so loudly it's like a horror film and a murder combined and the trusty earplugs have offered some relief.

Apparently 58 per cent of Gen Z have experienced hearing loss of some sort (likely due to headphone misuse and more noise exposure) and a lot of people do seem to suffer from tinnitus. I cannot imagine what an awful thing that must be to live with.

Proprioception

Apparently, there is another sense in addition to the standard five (not the sixth one, because that's already taken. The sixth sense is where you seem to know something without using any of the other senses). I do like to think humans are more than the sum of their five senses. So, I am going to call this other sense the seventh sense. It is *proprioception* and is an apparent awareness of the position and movement of the body. I think this one has worn off for me as I often don't know where my foot is.

Hair

Hair changes colour, gets thin and goes grey, but it also has the temerity to grow elsewhere, like on your chin, whilst your pubic hair is falling out. This redistribution seems more for comedy purposes than anything else. Good news, though – various online outlets will flog you a pubic wig which is called a *merkin*.

Sleep

Sleep can be severely curtailed as you age unless you have some sort of chemical help, by which I mean sleeping tablets. Some people who don't agree with tablet-induced slumber say, 'Be more positive, you get a few more hours in the day.' Yes, a lot of the time that will just be a few more hours to feel like shit.

Skin

Skin gets quite saggy and wrinkly as you get older – said she, stating the bleeding obvious – but the appetite for Botox and fillers these days can have a deteriorating effect as you age. One of the long-term effects of fillers is something called 'pillow face'. Inappropriately I laughed when I read that. Apparently, it's a puffy look that distorts natural contours. I reckon I can manage that on my own.

Healthcare

OK, not part of the human body, but it is another thing that, in my opinion, seems to decline as you age. In the (g)olden days, what were called 'geriatricians' were flourishing and oversaw all the illnesses of old age. These days, because of patient choice, and people living longer, a lot of issues are dealt with by specialists. This seems to mean that, instead of one doctor treating all your needs, you see more specialists, and the proliferation of different conditions in old age means that some older people may have so many appointments they don't have time to do much else. If in a relatively short space of time you're having a follow-up for your haemorrhoids, a hearing test, a wound dressing, a colonoscopy and an X-ray, will you actually want to do anything else except lying down and groaning a bit? A friend's dad had approximately seventeen appointments in the space of three weeks! This is all very well if going to see a doctor is one of your hobbies, but it isn't one of mine, although I suspect it may be in the coming years. Perhaps it's a good idea to have a health speciality bingo card and see if you can eventually tick them all off.

Another element of self-care health-wise is that it's good to be an average type. I used to think running long distances was the epitome of good health until someone I knew who ran marathons found themselves having to have a hip replacement in their mid-forties. And it's for that reason I gave up marathon running as opposed to running for a Marathon (now re-named 'Snickers' so, pointless antique joke).

Falling Over

The biggest danger when you get to a certain age is falling over. The second biggest danger is watching out for 'falling over' morphing into 'having a fall', because then consigning you to Old-Person-Cliché-Land has begun. When does this happen? Well, as a child you always 'fall over', but as you edge through adulthood, your progress towards 'having a fall' becomes ever more imminent.

Apparently the transition point is 65, which means I'm past that but still refuse to own it. Some people say if you need a hand getting up, you've 'had a fall'. Or you could just be drunk. I might try 'fall down' as a personal choice. 'I fell down' is all right, isn't it? Even better if you've got a cold because then you can chant, 'Atishoo! Atishoo! I fell down,' and tell everyone the apparently false origin of the nursery rhyme 'Ring a Ring a Roses'. It isn't about the bubonic plague, but don't let that get in the way of a good story.

And, of course, when you're older, because your bones are a bit weedy and thin, they break more easily. If you are very old, breaking a bone can be a gateway to disaster. A whole sequence is set in motion, which many elderly people fail to escape from. This may involve your treatment being severely curtailed because you cannot, for example, have an anaesthetic to reset things because you are too old. Or you may be considered unsafe at home or in a residential home that cannot offer any medical cover.

This is what happened to my dad. After it being too unsafe for him to live in his flat alone because he was wandering about at night and playing bumper cars in the car park, we reluctantly made the decision for him to be transferred to a residential place. We all held our breath, but it was wonderful and he loved it. The staff were brilliant and he got on well with everyone, spent his days watching films, reading the paper and loving the food. He also seemed a bit pissed off when people visited, because we interrupted whatever he was doing, so no change there. I like the thought of this. So often we family members feel so guilty about abandoning our relative in a home, but he couldn't wait to get rid of us, especially if a great film was on.

Then one night he fell down, and got carted off to hospital. This meant he could not return to his familiar place due to inadequate nursing cover. Instead, we had to move fast and the only place available on the day the hospital wanted to discharge him was very posh with beautiful furnishings (not really him, I have to say). We decided to try it for the weekend, arrived around midday, and were helping him get settled into his room when someone trundled through the door with a drinks trolley! Never one to turn down a drink, my dad accepted a huge glass of sherry, knocked it back in one and immediately his head dropped onto his chest, and he appeared to be unconscious. 'Bloody hell,' I thought, 'they've killed him already!' He then started to snore loudly and eventually my brother and I managed to rouse him and decided that this was probably not the best place for him.

Sometimes it's not just about fresh flowers and a beautiful setting looking out onto rolling hills, it's about what you're used to. In fact, when my dad passed out it was probably the shock of having a drink which was more refined than a pint of beer. And he had never used a posh napkin in his life!

My 'Fallings Down'

We've all done it and hopefully, providing we weren't badly injured, been able to laugh at ourselves. Please indulge me, as I whizz through my favourite fallings over (or is it 'falling overs'?).

For many years in a row our family would go away to the same place in Devon and stay with other families/friends/relatives – up to thirty-five of us, in cottages around a cobbled farmyard. Idyllic, most of the time. I was wearing Crocs one day, the cobbles were wet and I slipped and fell over backwards, hitting my head on the stones. Anyway, I opened my eyes, at least some seconds later. No one had spotted it, thank God, but my head really hurt. And just to add insult to injury, a few weeks later, a big clump of my hair fell off my head, and I had a lovely bald patch that took months to grow back. Happy days.

More recently, I fell down twice and that was because I was dragging my feet, mainly because I am lazy rather than tired. The first time I was, ironically, on my way into a GP surgery, and it was very early in the morning and dark. Of course, I wasn't looking where I was going and tripped over a very shallow kerb. I would have seen it if it had been higher, so have always viewed that kerb as an ambush device to give the CCTV monitors a laugh. So over I went, plummeted down like the proverbial sack of potatoes, going splat onto the tarmac. I put my hands out for fear of damaging my beautiful face and not getting any more modelling jobs, so my hands and knees took the brunt of it. I must admit by that point in my life I wasn't quite the sprightly elf I used to be, so it took me a bit of a while to notice there was a man standing right in front of me, just observing my graceful dive, at which point he said to me, 'Are you all right, love?' 'Yep, absolutely fucking great, thanks, mate, and congratulations, mister, for just standing there and not even offering to help, you useless piece of crap.' Unfortunately, it came out as, 'Yes, fine, thanks.'

The second time, I was fortuitously outside an A&E department with my daughter and her boyfriend, tripped over my feet and splatted again. And I will say, hats off to them for not pissing themselves laughing. Well, not actually in front of me anyway.

So how do you keep people safe and stop them injuring themselves and breaking a bone when they fall over? Well, having no stairs is a good start, which is why many people decide to move away from stairs to a bungalow. There are also several steps between your own place and a residential home with varying levels of supervision, from a warden, who will eventually find you in a heap beside the toilet, to gadgets which monitor your degree of uprightness.

My Fall Prevention Protocol

There are several ways to deal with preventing falls.

Clutter

It goes without saying that you need to keep an older person's living area clutter free. And what do most older people's homes have in them? Yes, it's loads of clutter! However, it's not what those people would call clutter. To them, this 'clutter' is made up of cherished belongings they have collected or been given over the years; unless you want to have a tug of war over a great number of them and seriously disorientate the person in question when they realize their home has been converted to something more reminiscent of a minimalist paradise, you may need to think again. Personally, I would love this, but I doubt most people would.

So, if the 'clutter' cannot migrate into a skip without a fist fight, I'm sure I have seen some inflatable-suit type things that immediately fill with air if there is any swift movement towards Planet Earth, but this could just be a weird dream. So, short of carpeting their houses with pillows, tying them to the bed or having someone to follow them round and catch them whenever they list to port or starboard, there needs to be something much simpler. I wouldn't mind some fun inflatable suits, like a dinosaur or a Father Christmas suit, and that would entertain my family enormously too, but what's the postman going to say when you answer the door dressed as a panda or in a ballerina fat suit? Which reminds me, I assume that if you are somewhat well padded yourself, you come into your own as far as falling is concerned.

Fall alarms are a thing too, I believe, and they are a good idea if they go through to a monitoring centre. I suppose cameras are a good thing as well, although we all know that, sadly, they are sometimes employed by relatives in care homes when it is felt that they might be needed to safeguard against poor nursing care or petty crime, which we cannot deny is a thing.

Falling Over Properly

If you do fall, just before you get stuck in, there is advice on how to fall properly. Who knew? First of all, if you do not want to break a bone in your face (and who does?), apparently if you turn your face away from the direction of the fall and sort of tuck it in as far as you can towards your neck, that might help. However, falls don't happen quite in the neat, predictable way you want them to, so you've got to remember this *as* you fall, and you won't have long. People also tense up before they fall and if you can possibly remember this as well: you need to *relax* your body as much as you can so you fall in a heap rather than like a concrete statue. Please don't sue me if this goes wrong, it's not my own advice, it's from some American bloke who looks like he isn't due a fall for about another thirty years.

Another little tip which may be quite difficult to achieve, is, if you are going to fall over, perhaps you could only do it when it's been snowing. Obviously this is quite difficult to facilitate as it doesn't snow that often. Last time it snowed quite heavily in London was, I think, 2018/19. I was out with my daughters (aged 16 and 17 at the time) and had the most inappropriate footwear on. They were not exactly slippers but they had no grip on them at all. Got out of the car, fell over; got up, fell over again; got up, fell over again. Got up and got back in the car. As far as my daughters were concerned that was the best comedy I'd ever done and I was delighted to entertain them. I should add that I didn't hurt myself at all and would recommend snow as a very effective cushion. Then again, I wouldn't have fallen over if the snow hadn't been there, so what am I even talking about? Elderly brain strikes again!

Staying Active

Keeping active in old age seems to be very important and activities are an opportunity to not let yourself metamorphose into The-Blob-That-Never-Moves, which I fear is the blockbuster movie I'll be starring in if I'm not careful.

Ruling out the obvious like the javelin, high jump, marathon running, pole-vault and rugby, does leave older people with some slightly less strenuous activities to take part in.

Aquafit

There are exercise sessions which do seem to be specifically aimed at older people. For example, there is something called Aquafit, which, although it is open to all ages, tends to be entirely populated with older women. I think this is probably because it is not quite so harsh on the deteriorating bone structure. Theoretically, Aquafit is open to men and women, but so far, I have only seen a man appear once for a session and after that he was never seen again. I'm not sure anyone in the group did anything identifiable to discourage him from returning. Maybe he felt the harsh gaze of many rheumy eyes boring into his back and decided not to bother. I always go to Aquafit with a friend who is a doctor – handy if I have a cardiac arrest in the pool, although she is a gynaecologist, so perhaps the best I could expect is an emergency smear. I have noticed, on occasions, the 12-year-old lifeguard doing a head count as soon as we get in the pool. Presumably this is on the off-chance that we don't all surface at the end. I'm afraid I see any kind of group exercise as an opportunity to have a sociable catch-up with my friend and we tend to talk without drawing breath. Consequently, we do miss some of the instructions being barked at us (in a friendly way) by the instructor, and so I end up bouncing around doing a vague impression of what everyone else is doing.

Walking

Walking is always good exercise, apparently, and that includes us ancient crones. That is because you can decide on a pace and distance that suits you, and new research is appearing recently about how many steps you should do a day, how fast you should go, and each piece of advice seems a little bit more palatable than the last, i.e. shorter distances and fewer steps. I did do a very long walk for Comic Relief in 2016 and that was 140 miles from Hull to Liverpool. I just wanted to show people that it was possible for a gym-shunner such as myself to stagger up hill and down dale. And it was so rewarding to see my step count rise to 70,000 on a couple of days. Bit of an improvement on my normal 70. The only issue, health-wise, I had after the walk was heart palpitations, which I was told by a specialist would just naturally go away.

And finally, I do want to stress again that it's very important to keep your vision in good nick as many falls are because older people do not spot very important signs. Like one saying, 'Steep Cliff'.

OVERLY SPECIFIC SYMPATHY CARDS FOR THE GETTING ON

Sorry to hear the cat pissed all over your new slippers and you'll need to get them dry-cleaned as they're not washable.

So sorry to hear you dropped your hearing aid into the recycling bin (brown bins every other Wednesday) and the binmen have taken it, so you can't listen to Ken Bruce tomorrow.

My condolences that your grandson drove your new mobility scooter into the pond and Ted says it's going to cost a fortune to fix it.

Deepest sympathy that your husband only got you some reduced-price supermarket flowers for your birthday, and you can't smell them anyway because of your nasal polyps.

He may be gone, you may be sad,
But you didn't even like your dad.
Given he was 95,
It's a wonder he was still alive.
He had no friends, was often pissed,
And yet, 'he will be sadly missed'.

With sincere condolences for the loss of your peace and quiet since your husband retired.

So sad to hear you forgot to turn on the sprinkler and your lawn's gone brown.

So sorry both your granddaughters are very irritating.

CHAPTER THREE

The Rime of the Ancient Brain

You know how sometimes people describe others as 'old before their time'? This usually means a 14-year-old who likes old men's trousers and reading the *Financial Times* while their peers are out and down. Face down, that is, having imbibed, ingested, injected or projected their halloumi burger.

I'm not trying to argue that I was old before my time, although I was living on my own by the age of 17 in what we called 'a bedsit' in those days, and would now probably be called 'a spacious apartment'. This was in a tall house overlooking the pier in Hastings with a novel-worthy bunch of fellow bedsitters, including a Rastafarian guy who played brilliant, loud reggae all day, five Korean chefs, a single mother with a tiny baby and her mum who seemed mainly to sell cannabis. It was glorious.

These days, I feel for the poor unfortunates who are still residing with their parents up to their mid-thirties as they struggle to afford a place you could fit into a wheelie bin, particularly in the London end of the UK. In fact, people are having to live longer purely so they have more time to save up for their own place.

I was forced to be old before my time and manage my own life, which included working in the Civil Service, returning to school a couple of days a week and otherwise being off my face. So, in human years my brain is 68 years old, but who knows how old it is in experience years. Probably about a hundred. I do feel like it's taken a battering throughout my life. I've used it too much and it's worn out, like an old sock that's been through the washing machine too many times.

I studied neuropsychology at university and found it fascinating. Don't panic, I'm not going to lay out the principles of the course that I did, because I can't remember a bloody thing about it apart from the odd snippet of stuff that stuck in my head, like the fact that electroconvulsive therapy (ECT) was discovered by an Italian doctor who noticed that many people who had epileptic seizures were a lot more cheerful afterwards. (That's not quite how he put it, btw.) Hence the use of electric shocks to simulate seizures for people with depression. Still used today, but much more targeted to very specific conditions.

The brain has always been largely uncharted territory with bits of the jigsaw added to each day by researchers all over the world. I couldn't hazard a guess at how complete that jigsaw is in terms of offering a completely comprehensive knowledge of the brain and how it works, but my best guess is 'not very'. Sorry to any experts out there adding pieces as we speak. Added to that, other factors are impinging daily on the brain and adding to the damage accrued throughout one's life. Environmental damage, damage from playing certain sports, God knows what in the water supply, something or other in tins of tuna (heavy metals?), noise pollution (heavy *metal?)*. And those are just the ones that spring automatically to mind, which not much does these days.

So, I think I'd better stick to my own poor ageing brain as it sheds some of the functions it used to have, or at the very least, shaves a bit of definition off each year. Surprisingly, the adolescent brain structure can last well into the early thirties (and far beyond that in my case). And as I have neither the wherewithal nor inclination to give you a regurgitated blow-by-blow account of the brain's development, I'm going to launch into aspects of the way *my* brain has been coping against the onslaught of age, bearing in mind we're all affected in different ways.

I suppose the most difficult change for me is my memory. I was recently asked if I would take part in a podcast in which some tests were involved, including a blood test, and this would enable the host of the podcast to reveal during the recording of the show what my brain age was compared to my actual age. In the age-old tradition of burying my head in the sand, I declined. What if they discovered my brain age was 93 years or even older? I might as well book myself a slot at the cemetery now. I wouldn't mind finding out. Just not at the same time as all the people listening and watching. Most podcasts are 'visualized' these days too, which means you can't turn up dressed in a sack with no make-up on any more.

Anyway, my memory's always been a bit useless, whether that's because it genuinely is, or because I don't listen to what people are saying a lot of the time – not deliberately, but because I tend to drift off into my own thoughts, or 'daydream' as it was called when I was at school. (Daydreaming about becoming a comedian, obviously.) Since leaving school and home, I probably started to mistreat my brain a bit more with drink and drugs, including managing to have my drink spiked on a couple of occasions with LSD, or, as we used to call it then, 'Acid, man!' I am tempted to describe these charming incidents to you, but they are almost as boring as describing one's dreams or explaining to someone what happened in *The Traitors*.

Sorry, I can't resist it! I'll be quick.

Trip 1: Drink spiked at a party when I was about 16. All I remember is a plate of sandwiches, all of which had the face of Bob Dylan and were singing 'All Along the Watchtower'.

Trip 2: Drink spiked in a pub. Walking home on my own afterwards, saw a monk in a phone box swinging a dead cat backwards and forwards and then a bright pink illuminated coach mounted the pavement and I had to jump out of the way of the phone box. As I passed a garden, a pack of huge wolves all tethered to a tree, with slavering jaws, strained at their leashes in an attempt, I assume, to break free and eat me.

Ironically, current research is investigating the potential of LSD for treating depression. This would be with micro doses, not the full-blown experience or 'trip', as we scruffy semi-hippies called it. Just think, a 'trip' to the chiropodist could be so much more fun. Psilocybin has also been trialled for the treatment of depression. Psilocybin is probably better known as a component of magic mushrooms, so that's two substances that were highly illegal in my teenage years both being trialled therapeutically. 'Oh, how times have changed!' is a very old-lady thing to say, isn't it?

I think the trouble for most women, memory-wise, begins in earnest during the menopause, which, to be quite honest, for me was quite an uneventful experience. I decided to forgo hormone replacement therapy in favour of (drum roll . . .) nothing. For some reason I wasn't sure I really felt the need for HRT. I was absolutely knackered all the time anyway and had very few symptoms.

More recently, 'brain fog' has set in with a vengeance and it's impossible to know why it's got so bad. There are loads of things that cause brain fog and reading through the far-too-long list I thought, yep, could be any of those or all of them. Added to that, a lot of people think that brain fog is a figment of people's (by which I mean women's) imagination. I do remember some poor female politician on the news completely drying up during her answer to a question and thinking that it was very unprofessional, then of course realizing much later what was going on and feeling sorry for her.

It's quite a tricky thing to disguise brain fog, but in my stand-up I have had to find ways round it and it is very wise to have a handy phrase at the ready to distract the audience, like 'Fire!', while you get yourself together. I think my big problem with stand-up is that I have always constructed jokes which have had to be delivered in a very particular way or they don't work, and saying, 'Oh bollocks, I've forgotten the punchline,' doesn't really do the trick.

In many cultures the menopause signals the start of a new phase in a woman's life, so for those women it gives them more freedom and they can stop worrying about potential pregnancy. In other cultures, it is the signal for women to prepare themselves for hot flushes (in the UK) and hot flashes (in the US). Women are so much more open about all things menstrual these days and this is a

GOOD THING. When I were a lad, if someone even alluded to 'women's things', at least three people in the room would faint.

In my days at school, misunderstanding about 'unpalatable things' was rife. The teachers were old-school and wanted to couch everything in language that didn't sound too rude. I remember after a lesson on periods – which I was absolutely horrified by, may I say – I went home and told my mum what we'd been taught and said the equivalent of, 'Well, at least we only have one of those period things. Imagine if they went on any longer?' She then had to solemnly inform me that the phrase 'once a month' had been omitted. I was devastated. Although it is possible I just didn't hear that nugget of essential information, as I was not famed for my intense concentration skills.

Women can now have babies at whatever age they care to, and if we're honest, most women aged 80 and over have not taken advantage of the door that has been opened by scientific progress. That's because women know it's hard enough looking after babies when you're 20 years old, let alone four times that. Many men don't know this, least of all the 90-year-olds on their fifth wife who generally, I would assume, don't have to get up at 3 o'clock in the morning to do their parenting bit.

I don't think Covid did people's brains any favours, and that is the understatement of the year. The net result of Covid for many people was social isolation, missed school, working from home (which many loved but large numbers hated) and, for many, mental health issues. We were unable to visit anyone properly, a common but heart-breaking phenomenon, particularly for those, including myself, who had seriously ill loved ones. Along the way there were so many experiences none of us had had before, nor knew how to cope with.

Doing and watching stand-up comedy on Zoom (remember that?) and not being able to know if anyone was laughing was just plain weird. And recording radio shows, with very little ability to make out individual voices, with everyone talking over each other was a whole lot of fun, let me tell you. On one show an exasperated sound technician shouted at the top of his voice, 'Will everyone just shut the fuck up!' We did. Unfortunately, I don't think that contribution went out on air.

My cognitive function took a bit of a hit during Covid and increased the amount of whatever the opposite of grey matter is. For that reason, I tend not to go on quiz shows any more, because even though I know I know some of the answers, I always prevaricate for ages about whether they're right or not. Also, my reaction time is that of a sloth. If there is a buzzer involved, I visualize the members of the charity I'm raising money for with their heads in their hands, as I reach for it ten minutes after everyone else. I think I've probably disappointed a few charities that way.

Quizzes are a nightmare too if you're very competitive,

and I hate to admit it, but I am. That is the problem of being the middle child with two brothers who used to feel it was their job not only to beat me at everything, but also to get me into trouble as often as possible. I can't remember why, but when I was about seven years old my mum and dad had to nip out for twenty minutes, leaving us with dire warnings about what would happen if they came back and discovered any visible evidence of 'mucking about' – quite high up in the charge list of Brand children criminal behaviour. They hadn't been gone five minutes when my brothers dared me to jump out of the kitchen window into the garden. It took a while to persuade me, but I couldn't resist a challenge, especially not from them, and was unfortunately caught virtually in mid-air as my parents' car appeared round the corner much earlier than predicted and I was rumbled. That incident didn't have a happy ending for me. I seem to remember being asked the question, 'So, if they told you to jump off a cliff, would you do that?' I tried to plead extenuating circumstances, but that was thrown out by the judges, unfortunately.

And so, in some ways, I am quite pleased to be free from the horror of competing and the ever-present looming fear that I might say something so ridiculous it would end up in *Private Eye*'s 'Dumb Britain' section, my appalling gaffe being preserved for posterity.

Many websites for the older population who are losing their minds recommend playing word games every day to keep your brain sharp, but I'm not sure how effective it is. I love a word game, cryptic crossword or those fiendish tests at Christmas in the broadsheets, when you feel like Einstein if you get even one right. I used to feel the same about getting a question right on *University Challenge* many moons ago, but these days it's more like a quiz for 12-year-olds.

So, if you have a bad memory, what's the best thing to do? These days it seems much easier than it used to be.

Making a list is a good if obvious start. I always start one, forget about it and start another one. So don't have more than one list. Sometimes I find three lists for the same day, and they have some of the same crossovers on them like 'FFS, don't make another list'.

Most people under the age of 'whatever age you must be under to prefer putting stuff in your phone rather than writing it down' ignore this very practical advice. I know pen and paper is weirdly alien to you. However, one of my daughters makes lists on her phone and that makes no difference as to whether she remembers to do those things or not. She is known in the family dinosaur memory business as 'a chip off the old block'.

When you have completed something on your list, TICK IT OFF, so you don't worm the cat twice in a week.

I realize here I am probably teaching my grandmother to suck eggs. Another thing I forgot to put on my list.

The other rule I try to live by is if someone messages me (who turned that into a verb?), I message them back immediately. I think a lot of people don't like doing this, which may be why I never hear from them again. If you genuinely forget to reply to someone and find yourself in a situation that reveals your ineptitude or leads them to think you are old and unreliable, just lie. I was never very good at lying, but it is slightly easier using text. Try to make up whatever story gets you out of trouble in the most credible way. I can see I'm not going to have many friends left after this, but my friends stopped reading my books years ago. I know because very few of them got over 50 per cent in the exam afterwards.

As I've aged, there's no doubt that it's been harder to remember my jokes. I have been at a few events when I've had a very stressful week, and they're a stressful audience: think drunk solicitors over 50, or pissed-off engineers who pretty much managed an audible sigh of despair as I trudged onto the stage suffering from blanket brain. Occasionally, I'll get through a few minutes' worth of 'hilarious' jokes then can't remember what I was going to say next. This is reasonably easy to disguise on most occasions, but it isn't something that happened when I was a young(er), more competent performer.

Writing comedy is like writing this book. I have good days and bad days. Some days ideas will germinate and evolve into passable sentences, and on other days a limited selection of banal and imagination-free ideas will drift hopelessly around in my head and then reject themselves, because they are neither interesting nor funny. And it's impossible to know which days are going to be which until they happen. Anyway, enough of me trying to trot out something about 'entertaining'. There are many other areas of my life in which my brain is doing a bit of a Homer Simpson 'doh!' at things that I was previously competent at. Ultimately, as people get older/mature, their brains will age in their own unique way. As my memory was always quite bad, it's sometimes hard to tell how much is ageing and how much is just me being generally rubbish at being organized.

Let's finish with motivation. From my experience, as we age, motivation to get up in the morning and 'attack' the day wanes somewhat. My motivation certainly goes on holiday often and I find myself wondering if it will ever be ready for action and return soon. However, if it doesn't, I won't be too worried, because all this stuff in the press about having an active life when you're older has made me feel tired. And if you do feel the need to resist all the exhortations to get out there and do one-handed press-ups or skydiving, resist them if you want to. No point putting yourself at risk at this time of your life. Or for some people the opposite may be true. Some of you out there might think, 'What have I got to lose now?' Yep, I can see that's a good point. Have a lovely time canoeing along a piranha-infested river in South America. See you when you get back. There are some tricks you can come up with to convince yourself you need to do less, like telling yourself your house looks interesting and quirky when, in fact, it looks like the proverbial bomb has hit it. But providing it doesn't smell like a compost heap and you don't have mice burrowing in your pillows, if it's reasonably OK, what does it matter? If it does smell like that, don't let anyone in, or just wear extra-strength patchouli perfume. That normally does the trick.

Here's a fascinating fact for you to forget. Although the brain is only 2 per cent of our body mass it uses 20 per cent of our daily calories, which sounds mad, doesn't it? So don't forget when you're eating wine gums: 2 for you, 8 for your brain.

Thinking of my own ageing brain has made me wonder what the future holds for the internet generation in terms of how their brains will age. I have to say that it doesn't look very positive. There is a viral social media expression, 'ageing like milk', which refers to another current Gen Z expression: 'brain rot'. Brain rot refers to the mental decline which results from Gen Z consuming endless low-quality internet content, leading to jumbled thoughts and intellectual emptiness. Well, even though *I've* most definitely got jumbled thoughts and I'm intellectually empty, it doesn't bode well, does it? Gen Z can't all put their brains in a fridge.

And it's not just an internet-coined phenomenon, because research has backed it up and it seems the cognitive impact of short-form video consumption is directly linked to cognitive functioning, including poor planning, memory issues and reduced attention span, and results in structural changes in the brain. Add to this doomscrolling and information overload and you are not going to be a happy bunny.

Having arrived at a somewhat negative ending for this chapter, I realize I haven't been entirely fair or balanced, and that's because old people are *meant* to slag off young people – it's our job. However, I have to confess, the younger generation are pretty clean-living compared to my lot. They're not drinking nearly as much as the semi-conscious hordes that have gone before them, and they're keeping drug consumption to a minimum as well – ish. So there is definitely space in their youthful brains to contend with a bit of social-media-induced brain rot. Besides, some of them are getting our old drugs carefully administered on prescription, which leaves lots of space free in the cerebral cortex for a bit of fun. And to quote the, by now, ancient musical combo The Specials: 'Enjoy yourself, it's later than you think.'

CHAPTER FOUR

To Infirmity and Beyond

If you could live a little or a lot longer beyond and above the average lifespan, would you? It's a difficult question to answer, given that it would be based on so many variables. If you knew which genetic timebombs were coming down the line (Grandma's arthritis, Dad's depression and, God forbid, Auntie Beatrice's personality, identifiable more by its absence than anything else), would you do anything about it? And what are the features that might make you tailor your decision to whatever you found out?

A handful of people are appearing out of the woodwork and trying to come up with a plan for extending their lives and avoiding the appealing prospects of the crumbling body. What do these people have in common? Well, most of them are loaded and a lot are American.

Let's take longevity-seeking tech-bro Bryan Johnson as an example. You may have got wind of him already, but if not, he's a bloke who wants to live for ever and aims to:

Stop self-destructive behaviours
Neutralize ageing
Come up with an anti-ageing protocol

Bryan has styled his project 'Don't Die' – the mantra of most stand-up comedians and not always very successful.

Bryan states, 'The gym is my happy place.' Yep, me too, mate, and he is in the 99th percentile for best muscles and appropriate amount of body fat. Not me too. Bryan takes fifty-four pills in the morning and thirty-four later in the day and apparently, for every twelve months that passes, he only ages eight months. He is 48 years old, but (wait for it), his rectum is only 18. Crikey! He's knocked thirty years off his rectum age and I think has possibly passed those thirty years on to me while I was asleep. I suppose he has to tell us, as it's not a question I often see on application forms.

Bryan has a son called Talmage from whom he milks various substances which will enhance his youthfulness. Looking back on this sentence, that sounds very unpleasant. I should have specified I mean blood plasma. He also has some from his dad as a multi-generational plasma exchange is a GOOD THING apparently.

Bryan thinks we have lost touch with basic self-care, and we can't stop eating shit. He's not wrong there, but his methods of rect(um)ifying this issue are where he loses touch with 99.9 per cent recurring of the medical bods. Bear in mind he is a squillionaire and he can afford to spout bollocks if he wants, because enough people listen without crying. Being absolutely minted makes all the difference. As he very graciously acknowledges: 'Not everyone has the resources to do this.'

There is no doubt that Bryan does take some risks with his body too. He has used a drug called Rapamycin for several years which has shown some signs of being anti-ageing, but the side effects have defeated him, not because he now looks like a 90-year-old, but because they are difficult to tolerate. At least his rectum is only 18, but he probably doesn't get much of a chance to show it off.

I don't know what kind of food he eats but it looks like a fruitcake explosion covered with mushy peas and oxtail soup, yum! The nicest thing you could say about the food is that it also looks very boring, and how many years does being bored shitless add on to your life?

Bryan grew up in the Mormon Church and had big problems with it, so that's one big tick in favour of his sanity. However, his big Don't Die project really began when he sold his company and left religion. He states, 'Removing the mind' was 'the best thing ever'. And that was when Bryan lost his, possibly. But I rather like the mindless Bryan, I have to say. He seems a slightly more empathetic character and certainly loves his son Talmage to bits. Talmage himself also appears surprisingly well-balanced and, at the time of writing, is about to head off to university, neatly escaping the more innovative aspects of Bryan's project, like being milked.

Meanwhile Bryan has been to Honduras, because a small island off the coast allows youth seekers to go there and do a bit of gene therapy, which is illegal elsewhere. Bryan has a lovely assistant and/or girlfriend. Can't tell which. Anyway, she's called Kate. Bryan is ready to dive headfirst into gene therapy despite the fact that Kate has misgivings about it. Rightly so. Surely unsupervised gene therapy is asking for trouble. We won't know until Bryan turns into an otter. Apparently, though, the two guys who set up the gene therapy facility (one hippie and one 11-year-old boy with a moustache) say that their gene therapy is at least reversible.

Bryan is spoken of as being a sort of 'Health Jesus'. I seem to remember Jesus brought people back from the dead, so he was very much a Health Jesus himself. It goes without saying that in an NHS-free America, if Bryan's remedies for our future extended lives and improved health actually do work, vast numbers of doctors in the US will have less to do and earn fewer dollars and might be mighty miffed by this. Bryan Johnson's attempts not to die will hopefully (in Bryan's world), be rolled out to the larger population, but obviously only the massively minted ones. Who wants the less well-off to live longer lives? Well, me for a start, but only if they want to!

I am thoroughly ambivalent about this, not that

anyone's offering me eternal life since I pissed off our local vicar when I was a child. I'm not even sure what eternal life really is, sounds hideous to me. Given how much the world has changed since I was 20, I can barely function practically, given the advances in technology which effectively shut me out of communication with the cool kids. In fact, I can hear my daughters laughing at me now, just because I used the expression 'cool kids'.

It seems to me that the older you get and the further away you move from the zeitgeist, the less society seems to rate you, despite the fact that many healthy, fitter, older people hold up the lollipop lady and charity shop staffing levels. Sure, some of them sit in great big houses on their own and refuse to move into a shoe box, while others need to be dragged, kicking and screaming, from their houses and plonked into residential care when they can no longer cope, of which more later. Back to eternal life.

Let's just balance Bryan Johnson out with a woman who similarly wants to live for quite a bit longer than most of us do. Her name is Kayla Barnes-Lentz, and she runs a wellness company and is the most measured woman in the world. That doesn't mean all her decisions are very thoughtful, it means people are constantly recording aspects of her potential long life. This statement is on her website, so I'm not quite sure how accurate it is. Her area of expertise is biohacking which is 'technology-driven clean living designed to promote health and longevity'. Sounds like a right laugh. She wants to live to 150. Why?

She is married to another 150-wannabe called Warren. Just to give you a brief idea of her day: Kayla wakes up at 5 a.m. (She'll be doing that without any help by the time she hits 135.) She somehow manages to control her body temperature with a mattress that also ensures she has proper sleep. Yawn. It's nice for her that her mattress is such an ally. I, on the other hand, have an uncomfortable mattress that likes to remind me I'm getting old by making my back hurt so that I wake up frequently, which also has the added bonus of making me look very haggard as well.

She then gets up and optimises her mind and body using pulsed electromagnetic field therapy. Don't we all? It's supposed to stimulate the cells. I do that with a cup of tea. Oh well, each to their own. I bet Warren's popping out the back for a beer and a smoke while she's doing that. Then she checks various bits and bobs of information about the old ticker, how decent her sleep is and then reads her horoscope. Well, maybe not that last one.

I think my favourite part of Kayla's day is her oral care routine. Here we go, brace yourselves . . .

She also indulges in something called 'oil pulling' with oil that is 'ozonated'. Thank heavens for that! God forbid she should use something most of us have heard of, like cooking oil. She then brushes her teeth and scrapes her tongue. Sadly, we're not told what she actually scrapes it with. I like to imagine her with a mini plasterer's trowel. Then normality returns for a very brief visit and she cleans her teeth, woohoo! There's also some 'light therapy' . . . yep, no idea either. And to think some of us just have a cursory couple of minutes with some toothpaste and an ancient toothbrush.

Kayla's day continues with a sunrise walk and an organic breakfast, followed by a cold-water plunge. Then she and her beloved take turns in a hyperbaric chamber. Does anyone else feel mildly suicidal yet?

Dinner is at 4 p.m., and Kayla says this is usually fish, beef and a big ole salad with cruciferous vegetables, whereas my veg are usually crucified. Poor old Kayla can't even have a proper coffee without adding a whole load of healthy stuff like creatine and colostrum. What's wrong with sugar? She is in bed by 9, but not before she's exposed herself to red light after sunset, whatever that means.

I'm sorry – ironically, I've lost the will to live, so I refuse to talk about Kayla any more.

A recently coined term 'longevity fixation syndrome' seems to be a potential fit for people like Bryan and Kayla. This describes the anxiety-driven obsession with living for as long as possible, and the numbers affected are rising. Some people seem to be so absolutely welded to their diet and exercise plans that any deviation from them causes a huge amount of distress. In fact, I read about someone in America who became so upset that his meal was served with pitta bread instead of crudités that he had what he describes as 'a breakdown'. I think he had become so obsessed with monitoring his food closely and recording every bodily function that this was the final straw and he sought treatment.

Ironically, the clinic he sought help at was one in Switzerland and, as we know, Switzerland is known mainly in this country for representing recourse to a very different sort of clinic. It also seems very unfortunate that the CEO of said clinic happened to coin the term 'longevity fixation syndrome', given that the clinic offers treatment for this very syndrome. This would be all well and good if the treatment didn't cost a staggering £88,000 a week, way beyond all but about seventeen people's reach.

Just to introduce a showbiz element into this, it's perhaps interesting to note which celebs are dipping a toe in the longevity fountain of youth. For example, Orlando Bloom has tried filtering his blood for microplastics, and Jennifer Aniston uses peptide injections for skin rejuvenation. Time for me to have an apple, I think!

There is a charming line in George Orwell's book *1984*: 'If you want a picture of the future, imagine a boot stamping on a face, for ever.' This is how I think I might possibly feel if I had Kayla's life and was destined to endlessly watch reruns of seventies sitcoms on one of those old-codger channels. Extending life, apparently, is all about lifestyle, healthy diet, regular exercise and avoiding harmful habits like smoking, excessive alcohol and illegal drugs. All the fun things if you're my type of person.

So, you could be sitting in your residential home with a local choir singing 'Live Forever' to you, infinitely preferable to something like 'It's a Long Way to Tipperary', which by then will mean nothing to the captive aged.

Who Wants to Go to the Lovely Place?

Many religions promise eternal life, and I do envy people who are convinced of the certainty of an afterlife. How brilliant to go swanning around safe and secure in the knowledge that when the time comes for you to shuffle off, paradise is waiting for you, but if it isn't, by the time you get there you won't even know anything about it. Result! There will just be blank nothingness, a bit like reruns of budget speeches from the 1950s.

Who Doesn't Really Want to Go to the Fiery Place?

I'm not going to dwell on the Bible for very long . . . I'm not that kind of gal! I remember thinking as a child that it wasn't for me and marvelling at the fact that anyone could have got anything out of it. The medieval language, the virtual absence of women in the Old Testament apart from baby machines and the odd temptress.

Let's briefly outline Hell. It's a place of punishment and destruction, fire and fury, although it is not made clear exactly how that would work. There is plenty of weeping and gnashing of teeth apparently. I know what weeping is and, fair enough, Hell is full of unhappy people who are pretty damn pissed off to be there. As for gnashing of teeth, can't say I've ever witnessed that and presumably older people in biblical times didn't have many teeth left to gnash anyway. Just as well these days as only very wealthy people can afford a dentist.

So, we can safely assume that Hell is whatever our modern equivalent is these days, and everyone has their own personal idea of what the very worst things in their (after)life could be.

I don't want to speak on behalf of older people, but to bring things up to date, let's just have a quick run through my top five ideas of Heaven and Hell for the more mature woman.

Heaven

1. Being as grumpy as you like, because that is an expectation.
2. Pretending I'm deaf as selectively often as I need to.
3. Wearing the same pants three days running because people expect you to smell anyway.
4. Not having to talk to anyone, because people think you're boring.
5. Staying in when you don't want to go out, and using old-person excuses like your 'lumbago's playing up' (whatever that is).

Hell

1. People going on and on and on about their gardens. I know lots of people love gardening, but . . .
2. People recognizing the back of your head as being attached to the rest of an old person when you are driving and treating you with a high degree of impatience, trying to get past you, tailgating you and being twats.

3. Pharmacists raising the volume in the chemist when you have asked for something embarrassing like extra-absorbent Tena Lady (for Secret Santa) and on occasions declaiming the bloody information at you, so the entire population can hear about your yeast infection.
4. Helping, nay forcing, you across the road when you just wanted to stand there for ten minutes staring at your feet. (All right, I made this one up.)
5. Thinking you're interested in things like flowers and babies.

The future is rushing towards us at an ever-faster rate, and the thought of dinosaurs existing for thousands and thousands of years with very little to do except eventually become extinct is beyond alien to us now. These days, innovations in our lives are happening so quickly, we can barely process them before the next, bigger, better version comes along, and one new piece of tech is ditched almost as soon as it's gone on the market. And, ironically, these innovations, rather than elucidating things, seem to make them obfuscatory. But maybe it's not that fast and it just seems that way as you age? Five-year-olds seem to cope perfectly well with them. Therefore, it is almost impossible now to imagine what old age will look like in the future.

Several films and TV shows in the past and in the current day have had a stab at it. As I've got older, I've often thought of a film called *Logan's Run* in which people are killed off when they reach the grand old age of 30, presumably to deal with over-population. That doesn't fill those of us in our late sixties with joy. Perhaps this sort of jeopardy would make the National Lottery a bit more exciting. I also remember a film called *Soylent Green* in which (mainly old) people are killed and made into food. I'll have a spoonful of Mavis with some mash, please.

We may scoff (not if we're anywhere near Soylent Green, mind you) but some futuristic films made many years ago do now have a certain prescience to them. *2001: A Space Odyssey*, in which the computer Hal goes rogue and starts making his own decisions, for example. Hmm, AI anyone? And as for *Alien*, a creature bursting forth from someone's stomach doesn't seem impossible now either, especially if you've been swimming in a river the water companies have disgorged anything into. At least there's some tech these days which will tell you the poo percentage of most stretches of water.

Who knows if future generations will look back on these times and see them as Utopian or desperately savage? But I think we will find that, as is common, there is a pecking order and the elderly will always tend to be right near the bottom of it, face stuck in a bowl of salted caramel Complan, if I have my way.

The *Doctor Who* TV series contained many ideas for unusual table lamps, for example, a brain in a dome (and not a very attractive one at that), which controls operations. We haven't quite got there yet, but we can certainly keep people alive who have no way of communicating with us, which presents us with the tricky question of whether it is cruel to keep this twilight life going. We still have a huge dilemma as far as euthanasia is concerned and one frequently hears the comment, 'You wouldn't let an animal suffer like that.' Unfortunately, a handful of people do treat animals like that and maybe they could be euthanized first just to see how it could all work. I hear many social commentators (not sports ones, thankfully) discussing ageing and the elderly, saying that society has got it wrong. This contentious area can never be fully resolved, as there are very overheated feelings.

So, are we living too long? Would we benefit from having a shorter life? I don't mean should we have snipers on the high street taking potshots at anyone who looks over the age of 90, but I do sometimes wonder if I lived to a very old age, would the last few years of my life be worth the hassle for me? Most people I discuss this with say things like, 'Well, as long as you've got all your marbles,' but I don't think it's that simple, because how do you decide how many marbles you need to live a fulfilling life? And, although older people are not really portrayed in that way, our views are not sought regularly apart from the important ones. (Old people, not views, that is!) After a certain age, in some people's eyes, one might just as well seek the opinion of a roomful of blancmanges.

Although I wouldn't advocate the possibility of allowing people to choose their time of death (not out loud anyway), I think there is a lot to be said for stopping being so squeamish about the whole subject and discussing it properly. Fine, if you change your mind at the last minute when the local vicar/policeman/undertaker is heading towards you with a stun gun or a sherry glass of cyanide, let us at least have a proper discussion about it. And we'll do that when we get to E for euthanasia in the Alphabet of Age.

MY ANTI-LONGEVITY PLAN

With respect to all those US-based longevity gurus doing their best to seek immortality, I think it's probably wise to plant my flag in the opposite camp. Here is the routine I will strive for:

Exercise

The gym is 'my unhappy place'. You might find this very hard to believe, but I find gyms terrifying. I can't even remember the last time I walked through the grim portals of one of those fetid torture chambers. I am not averse to group exercise per se, but it's that winning combination of competition, repetition and silent, yet obvious, judgement that does my head in.

My plan: Never go near a gym.

Diet

Having read a bit about how our diet can extend our lives, I had to go outside and have a bit of a scream. It seems many people favour intermittent fasting these days. I can see why this is valuable and I often like to leave an extra ten minutes in between breakfast 1 and breakfast 2. I'm sure it helps. I also hear tell of a strange phenomenon called 'eating windows'. No, it's not a circus act but the number of hours within which you consume all your calories for the day. Unsurprisingly, it's not twenty-four. A small eating window would be five hours or so early morning, whereas a larger more manageable one would be the size of the Brandenburg Gate. And finally, it is recommended by some that no salt or sugar WHATSOEVER is consumed. What a joyless existence that sounds, doesn't it? And so torturously long too, which is ironic.

My plan: It's far too late now to be worrying about changing my diet, so I won't.

Sleep

The sort of things you are advised to do to get a good night's sleep are to have a consistent routine, dedicate 30-60 minutes before bed to unwind, limit screen time, avoid heavy meals, don't work or watch TV in bed. Hahaha, I don't do any of these, but the irony is, when you get older, sleep, however much you wish for it, slips through your fingers.

My plan: Ignore the advice about sleep. Even if you try to start, it won't work now, anyway.

Meditation

Meditation is advised so that people can reduce stress, lower inflammation and live a longer life. I did try meditation many years ago when I was a student, but it seemed I couldn't manage to empty my brain of all the rubbish that was in it. I was hoping for a serene, calm, stress-free brain, but I couldn't stop thinking about random crap. Fail.

My plan: Meditation is obviously not for me so I'm going to read a book instead, but not one on meditation.

Moderation

Moderation to me is one of the most depressing words in the English language. I've never quite been able to get to grips with being a moderate person. Anyway, one person's moderation is another person's extreme. (All right, I just made that up.) I would be a moderate person if I could and have sort of tried and it's not for me.

My plan: I *might* try moderation in moderation, but I will start with a very moderate amount of moderation.

CHAPTER FIVE

Upper Crust or on the Breadline?

Although there aren't too many Bryan Johnson types around, it is generally true that rich people live significantly longer than poorer individuals (surprise, surprise), and studies show that the wealthiest can luxuriate in the knowledge that they can expect an extra decade of life and even longer periods of 'healthy' life, free from disability, due to better access to healthcare, healthier environments, nutrition and less stress. So, they get quantity and quality as well! Lucky rich people! However, it's a cliché to say so, but some wealthy people are the most miserable bastards I have ever met, and people with very little money, well, they're bloody miserable too.

You probably think I'm a hypocrite separating myself from the rich people and I can't deny it, but I've never been part of that inherited wealth, landed gentry sort of wealthy people, who I tend to think of as 'proper wealthy'. I've never owned a tiara, a shooting stick or a butler. I'm just a pleb done good. Obviously, it's lovely that my career took off, and I am so grateful. I have even tried to enjoy so many more people hating me. However, I suspect that the first half of my life before comedy had already set the agenda in terms of my longevity.

This gulf between 'most people' and 'the rich' was made very clear to me at a young age when I was at primary school in a little village in Kent called Benenden. Many people will not recognize that name but Princess Anne will, because she went to a very posh school in Benenden, predictably called 'Benenden School'.

The school was something like *Malory Towers*, which showcases a lot of 'jolly-hockey-sticks' types who hare around the many sports pitches on the coast of Cornwall with the backdrop of an imposing old building with towers, of course. Benenden schoolgirls played lacrosse, as did the *Malory Towers* mob, had acres of beautiful parkland and the obligatory swimming pool. It was only in the very long, private-school holidays that us plebs from the village were allowed to go up and use their pool. 'And very lovely it was too,' she said through gritted teeth. After getting a quick look at the advantages of a very posh school, albeit only in the school holidays, I continued onward in a series of state schools.

I think the main thing for me with private school kids was that although, as I said, I loved *Malory Towers*, I wouldn't really have wanted to go there. I would have missed my family and found it impossible to keep up appearances. I loved the village where I lived and wouldn't have found a sense of community in a private school where the prevailing wind was money and breeding for success. The same goes for the little I observed of the Benenden School pupils. I have always identified very strongly with state education and didn't ever feel comfortable around what I called 'the flicky-haired girls', who were always impeccably turned out. This was never possible for me in any sense of the word. I tended to have bits of food on my clothes, my hair was always a mess because I went to the 'salon of Mum' as a young kid and I gravitated towards disorganized people-pleasers with zilch sense of entitlement. I do realize I am lumping everyone at private school into the same clichéd group, but that's one of my many and varied faults. My family had set me on a non-girly, politically aware road and I have rarely deviated from that, despite the efforts of many a frustrated wardrobe person on various TV shows.

The difference between the facilities in state schools compared with private schools is vast. Well, playing fields are vast at private schools for a kick-off, if I'm not much mistaken, and the school will get stuck in straight away by exercising the children more effectively like ponies (and many pupils in private schools will have one too). Playing fields at state schools used to be a lot bigger until a certain (cherished by many/hated by many) prime minister called Margaret Thatcher (yes, her) came along. Her government encouraged local authorities to sell off school playing fields for development in the 1980s and this led to 10,000 playing fields disappearing. Glorious, I'm sure, for the developers, but maybe not quite so glorious for the children who missed out and had to play 43-a-side football to get their steps in.

So, an expensive education might have helped me live longer, if only I had had one, not to mention future networking in terms of earning opportunities, which also has a massive impact on life expectancy. It depends on how chaotic your life is and whether you choose to follow the route set in place by your parents. Going to a top university sets in place lifelong connections. Look at the Bullingdon Club at Oxford, for example, an all-male (naturally) group of students, some of whom followed each other into government or a perch somewhere at the top of society's power elite, and those connections allowed them into areas of earning and the best forms of living available.

I got a snapshot of this when I ended up going to Oxford. Oh, all right, it was to do a debate after I became a comedian. I was pitted against an entitled male student and honestly it was like going up against a seven-year-old child. It didn't help that his guest at the dinner beforehand was his mum, who took me to one side and asked me to be kind to her son who was proposing the motion. He was called something like Rupert and his opening salvo in a debate about feminism was, 'I know Jo Brand is a feminist because she's got hairy legs and she doesn't wash her hair.' Good God, what a sparkling debate that turned out to be. I'm afraid I felt moved to wipe the floor with him and remember very well his mother's thunderous expression as I bade Oxford University a relieved farewell. It seems highly likely that someone like 'Rupert' will end up living a much longer, healthier life than his poorer counterparts. I would like to wish whoever he got married to *very good luck indeed.*

Health

Wealthy people don't necessarily have better genes, although it's highly likely they do have better jeans. I've never been the sort of person that can spot an expensive piece of clothing from 10 metres like some people can. Would you know if something was a genuine Hermès bag, for example? I wouldn't and I wouldn't care either. They are a ridiculous amount of money. I saw one online called a 'Hermès 20 Faubourg' which was on sale for £190,000 and it was a second-hand one! I've bought a house for less than that. What is the matter with people?

Sorry, anyway, it goes without saying that healthcare differences can be a major advantage for the rich, although the main benefits, given the parlous state of the NHS, are quicker appointments. Unfortunately, the wait for NHS appointments is so long currently that people who can afford to are turning to private care to have quicker access to scans and tests, as well as a receptionist with a posh suit on who doesn't look stressed beyond belief and has had time to do her make-up. The same doctors work for both the NHS and private healthcare, although they obviously look a lot smarter and make sure their hair is combed when they're doing private work.

Private patients get a room to themselves with nicer food, although I must say if I was caught up in an emergency, it would be NHS every time because, to me, the care is better, although one might face the jeopardy of being in the corridor in a bed, or on a chair in A&E for very many hours. Added to this, there aren't any private A&Es in the country, anyway. Private healthcare, despite the advantages, does have some more major drawbacks other than no A&E departments. The word 'private' is a clue, because these companies are multiplying like amoebae (yes, I did Latin for a while at grammar school even if I didn't get to ride a pony). Of course, private health companies are driven by profit, so that if you seem to be in the market for chronic illness, they tend to back off and limit the amount of dosh they'll shell out for anything ongoing.

When I was a student nurse, I did do a shift in a private hospital and the only care I was called upon to offer while I was there was shaving a very imperious woman's legs (Rupert would have loved her). That kind of put me off the job for the rest of time.

Some changes have occurred over recent years that I think have created a problem for those who use the NHS for their GP service. I think having access to a GP you know and like is very important because of the continuity aspect of care, but these days, because of reorganization, mostly people will see a different GP every time they visit, and if you're an older person who saw the same GP for years, it can be unsettling. Gone are the days when people would have just one GP who also (can you even imagine it now?) would have visited them at home if they felt it necessary.

One lovely GP I had did not beat about the bush. I remember going to see her once, having not seen her for a while, and I had put on some weight. She asked me to get on the scales, which I did, and as she looked down to see how much I'd put on, she exclaimed, 'Fuck a duck!' Now that's the sort of honesty I like.

Teeth

Going to the dentist isn't what it used to be. I remember as a child the joy of visiting the dentist, the cheery atmosphere, the comfortable environment, the pain-free experience. Oh, OK, it wasn't quite like that. I remember my mum having a filling once and the dentist had not given her enough painkillers. When he started drilling, she cried out in agony. He had a lovely bedside manner: he just told her to shut up.

Even so, at least dentists then were free, gruesome as a visit to them could be. Nowadays there's roughly one NHS dentist per 3 million people. Yep, exaggerating again, but in some areas it's almost impossible to get an NHS dentist without going on a very long waiting list. This has led to people who can't afford private dentistry to take drastic measures. You may well have thought the old Laurel and Hardy type comedies in which someone tied their loose tooth to the bumper of a car and waited for it to drive off were hilarious, but unfortunately for a lot of people that is not far from the truth. Not only that, we also now have a separate sadistic person called 'a hygienist'. They *actually* tell you how to clean your own teeth and try to make you buy an electric toothbrush that costs quite a lot more than a normal toothbrush.

Americans have always believed we Brits have terrible

teeth compared to them. Well, let me just put that myth to bed. Research has shown it's actually the other way round, so get your own gnashers in order, guys. But I think it's safe to say, in conclusion, that wealthy people's teeth are far less likely to be in danger of being attached to the bumper of their Bentley.

Food

Do wealthier people eat better food than poorer people? In a word, yes. Along with all the other ingredients for a long, healthy life, diet is important. Being overweight is a threat to overall health and seems to be much less prevalent amongst the wealthy. This is because 'the wrong thing' is often so much cheaper than the right thing.

So, while we're here in the tricky realm of food, it's worth mentioning that the upper echelons of society do tend to eat a healthier diet as they can afford to buy fresh food and have better access to it. Lower-income households are much more likely to buy ultra-processed foods, designed to be addictive whilst sheltering under the banner of cheapness and convenience. The biggest problem with ultra-processed foods is identifying them, because they seem to be in so many different foods and the packaging does not go into detail in anything except a print unreadable to the naked eye. Eating these foods directly correlates to poorer health, especially in older age, and an entire generation of young people seems to have been set up for health issues later on, ensuring old age will be peppered with many trips to the doctor's surgery, which as we all know, at the moment is like trying to get into a Taylor Swift gig.

There was a golden era many moons ago when larger women were deemed wealthier and healthier too. Those days (Victorian times) are long gone, sadly, and we 'larger ladies' (I hate that phrase) have been consigned to weight-based discrimination. Unfortunately for me, I'm in the wrong era weight-wise, but in those days, once women married, they lost their wages, independence and almost certainly their minds. Oh well, you can't have your cake and eat it, I suppose, even though the person who came up with that phrase may have had their jaw forcibly wired up. Now that was a dieting phase that nobody misses.

It's interesting that attitudes can take an about-turn so easily. Thin women are admired these days not only for aesthetic reasons, but morally and health-wise too, because so many positive attributes are attached to thinness. Thin women are more self-controlled and more successful. So, if we turn to fat women, where do we start? Please feel free to join in with any general abuse you have heard. 'Not very bright', 'slovenly', 'lazy', 'aggressive', 'unattractive', 'murderous', 'satanic' and 'full up'.

In fact, one study found that a fat woman who lost a substantial amount of weight would see an income boost comparable to obtaining a master's degree. But what does that actually mean? You'd still get a job that required you just looking good rather than using your brain, surely?

I think as a stand-up, I had to be prepared for people heckling stuff about my weight, especially at places like The Comedy Store. On Friday and Saturday nights they had two shows. The second show started at midnight, so you can imagine what sort of advanced state of wasted the audience was in. A substantial number were never less than revolting. And that, dear reader, is why I am so flippant about my weight as I've had everything including the kitchen sink verbally slung at me and I couldn't really care less any more.

It does not help that women we (seemingly) admire in society are pretty thin, not to mention pretty and thin. The model Kate Moss's most famous quote is 'Nothing tastes as good as skinny feels', whereas Victoria Beckham has recently remarked that she thinks being thin is old-fashioned, although she seems not to have followed her own advice: 'Women these days want to be curvy and womanly.' Do we? Which women? I must have missed that memo. I'm not sure Victoria Beckham is down with the kids as we've gone right back to skinny quicker than you can say 'Pass me the celery', and certain celebs look positively emaciated. I did think I might try the charmingly named 'fat jab', but only so I could lose weight quickly and eat my way back up over Christmas.

It will be fascinating to see what weight-loss jabs do to the landscape of obesity over the next few decades. When these injections arrived in our lives recently, for a while they appeared to be the golden ticket to a healthier, more attractive life and a way of treating the huge societal problem that obesity has become with the rapid appearance of Type 2 diabetes. I worry that the so called 'fat jab' is not quite the saviour many imagined, as there do seem to be several unresolved issues with it. And it seems all wrong that unless you're extremely obese you can't get it prescribed on the NHS.

You might think it has to be taken for ever because as soon as you stop, you start eating everything within a 5-mile radius. However, if you do keep taking it, you run the risk of acute pancreatitis. 'No such thing as a free lunch,' seems a slightly inappropriate thing to say here, but it's true and I do know someone it's happened to.

The main promise of the jab is that it helps to reduce appetite. This apparently is because unhealthy food has a very loud voice. I know this to be true. Just the other day I was rushing around the house trying to get organized and I heard a voice. It kept saying 'Eat me!' and it seemed to be coming from a cupboard. I looked in the cupboard, and it was a packet of biscuits. Would not shut up until I ate them all.

Doughnuts shout louder than apples and, so far, it is difficult to work out just how many people suffer with this problem of 'food noise'. The concept has been around for about twenty years, but the food's been shouting louder for the last couple of years particularly. I believe the concept of food noise has replaced the very similar concept of 'comfort eating', which references those people who cannot stop thinking about food even when they're not eating it. But food mainly tends to address you when you're on your own, I find. If you're distracted enough by an activity or a conversation or similar, you tend not to dwell on food, apparently. And if you believe that, you don't know over-eaters. Why would I want a bath when I'm hungry? Or to read a book? They do realize, don't they (the torturers), that you can eat and do almost any distraction activity at the same time?

I feel I must confess here that I did go to Weight-Watchers once when I was a nurse but found being weighed in front of everyone was a bit more shaming than I'd imagined. Especially if you've put on weight that week. I felt like I was going to be executed. The only positive thing about it was that it cheered everyone up because it wasn't them. And you're standing there wondering what sort of expression to make for maximum effect. A sort of '*mea culpa*' pose, eyes downcast, or a defiant expression and raised middle finger? Anyway, it put me right off and I didn't go back after that.

Homes

Most wealthy people will grow up in a generally healthier environment, by which I mean everything around them is healthier. Well-off people will tend to have bigger, cleaner, dryer houses, whilst the much poorer sections of society will tend to live in more cramped, crowded, less well heated, occasionally damp houses, sometimes with the added horror of mould. They may also work in more cramped conditions, do multiple jobs, travel on public transport, where, let's face it, the likelihood of picking up some sort of virus is much higher. I realize here I am describing almost Dickensian conditions, but that is not far from the reality for many people. Until recently, no one had heard of 'houses of multiple occupation'. These are not particularly healthy environments to live in either. More poorer people will rent, as they can't afford to buy, rents will then increase and this puts them in a precarious position in terms of being settled for most of their lives.

Substances

And then there is the issue of harmful substances, which can be grouped together under the heading of smoking, drinking and drugs. Interestingly, although wealthier people, especially men, are likely to drink frequently and excessively, they have the cushion of a better diet, health-care and coping mechanisms, whereas for poorer people the harms are greater with a higher likelihood of binge drinking in deprived areas. As someone who got off my face regularly at university, I can't really see the point of moderation.

Would anything have stopped me smoking when I was younger, or even before I started? Difficult to say, but no, probably not. Because my home life was quite unstable, I found myself always doing the opposite to what I had been told, and then that habit became somewhat ingrained. I think health campaigns can only take you so far.

Had I become a world-class athlete, I think perhaps I would have thought about giving up smoking. However, although I was good at some sports – squash, for example (and, yes, a wag did once remark, 'Did you sit on your opponent?') – I wasn't brilliant at any sport. In fact, I was only pulled in if they couldn't find anyone else to do it. At my final school in Hastings, before I left home, I was commandeered to throw the javelin on sports day. And, I admit, I was not a well-behaved person. So, I was in the toilets having a quick puff before sports day kicked off. I lit one, blew out the match and put it back in the box. Well, I thought I had blown it out. Sadly not. The other matches in the box all caught fire at once and sort of blew up in my hand. The hand I threw the javelin with. Obviously I couldn't go and explain, so I ran it under the tap and went out to throw the javelin with my left hand. Of course it went about a metre. I didn't win. It got a good laugh though, so maybe that's when a comedy career started beckoning. Ultimately, nothing really stopped me smoking until I had children. That lasted a long time, but stress stepped back into my life, and it's been on and off since then.

CHAPTER SIX

Care Bots

In past times there was of course very little technical gadgetry available to help anybody with anything, least of all boring old people. Until Benjamin Franklin started messing about with lightning, there was no technical gadgetry whatsoever. Available aids for older people were mainly walking sticks, glasses and rudimentary wheelchairs, which of course are all still available today in a much more sophisticated form. And the idea of ear trumpets is glorious.

Ear trumpets appeared first in the seventeenth century and could be up to 24 inches in length. The most well-known ear trumpet user was Beethoven, who famously suffered from progressive deafness through his life. To the relief of many, aids for hearing have become increasingly discreet over the centuries, and currently are pretty much undetectable. Though ironically these days many much younger people are at risk of hearing damage or tinnitus because of the volume they listen to music at through headphones, or the volume at very loud gigs. I have to confess I do stick a pair of earplugs in if I'm off to something loud like fireworks. That's normally because the dog has borrowed my ear defenders. (And in true old-person style, I'd like to take this opportunity to ask why there have to be fireworks all year round? It's bloody annoying. Thank you for your indulgence.)

Many moons ago, older people didn't live nearly as long as they do currently, and so today's vast array of gadgets encompasses much older individuals with multiple needs.

As we age, the major issues in terms of how we manage our lives can be divided into physical and mental factors. Things we all once took for granted are now harder to do or impossible. There's no point me trawling through them all, because we pretty much know that what's coming down the line is a lottery.

The lucky ones who have looked after themselves will have some confidence that they might have prepared the groundwork adequately enough to escape a totally dependent old age. But there is a no man's land in between where predicted outcomes can become unexpected endings. This works both ways and all of us in the live-now-pay-later club harbour a secret hope that we will escape the clutches of the angry god of ageing.

So, who wants to be looked after by a robot in

preference to a human carer? Most people's immediate answer to that question I think would automatically be the answer 'human', especially older people in the present day. They will be of an age that they only remember the odd robot in sci-fi films and, like me, tend to think they are all vaguely human-shaped and speak with a Dalek voice, and who wants to chat with that about the price of fish?

A bit of me feels like I wouldn't mind being cared for by a robot as long as:

1. I could turn it off and back on again if necessary.
2. I could hit it with a small hammer occasionally or unscrew bits. (In a DIY sense, not a vindictive one).

I reckon we'd get on well, providing it didn't go rogue and try to kill me. Well, not unless I'd asked it to do that, anyway. And maybe in the future we will trust robots to make those sorts of decisions, who knows?

I think it's really important to separate the physical from the emotional here in terms of how willing potential recipients might be to receive care.

So, let's start with the physical side of caring for the elderly.

A Bot to Wipe Your Bum

One of the things I've never been keen on is the idea that carers who you probably may not even have met before, let alone know, could end up performing the most personal of duties in the day-to-day care of patients in residential facilities, and I can't really think of anyone I know who would feel differently to me. There is no doubt that carers, on the whole, are under such pressure as far as volume of work is concerned, that inevitably they will have to treat you as a job to be dealt with in the quickest possible time. Robot care seems a bit more private and dignified, providing the robot is not live-streaming toilet time on a YouTube channel for the entertainment of weird people. I'd be tempted to put a couple of sticking plasters over its little robot-y eyes, but then it wouldn't be able to see what it was doing and might wipe your handbag instead of your bum.

So there are drawbacks for both. Does anyone really trust technology these days? I bloody well don't. Who knows what it's up to?

I suppose one good thing about robots is they're going to be consistent in their approach, unlike carers. One would imagine robots will not respond to the prevailing atmosphere of an individual residential home. Some of them do seem to be very closed environments which are open to bullying, thieving and neglect. Would a robot end up mimicking the behaviour of the human staff or blow the whistle? It's far too early to ask that. There are lovely care homes where people are cared for and looked after very well. I am not denying that at all, but ignoring the bad ones does nobody any good, least of all the poor residents, many of whom don't have a voice.

At this point, I should perhaps say that I think it's very sad that so many relatives feel the need to put cameras in a relative's room to monitor behaviour of the staff, but it seems that this particular advance in technology is very necessary to catch unacceptable behaviour, from eating someone's KitKat to much more serious forms of abuse. Whistle-blowers don't seem to get a great press, do they? I've never really understood why they are viewed with such suspicion and antipathy. Some reasons for this are cited as threatening the organization's stability or violating implicit codes of loyalty. Stability of what? Loyalty to whom? If the organization is rotten to the core, they deserve all they get.

I tried to whistle-blow many years ago when I worked in a residential home for adults with learning disabilities, because of some quite appalling behaviour by some of the male staff. I complained to the head of the home, and he said as I was the last one to be employed, I should be the one to leave. Yes, I was gob-smacked, but only 17 years old and I didn't know what to do, so I just left, but now regret that hugely. I should have got my mum to go in all guns blazing, but that wasn't an option as by then I'd been 'invited' to leave home and we'd lost contact for a bit.

Given that many carers are enormously warm and conscientious, in comparison, robots do not seem like they'll promise much warmth in their interactions, but maybe I'm being unfair. Can you programme empathy into a robot? It doesn't work with people. And quite a lot of humans haven't got any to start with.

It seems so weird to me at the age of 68 that we are even discussing this issue of robot/human capabilities in the care world. Admittedly, robots are not properly up and running yet in the UK care sector. Other societies such as Japan, Korea, The Netherlands, Sweden and Germany are already well ahead of us. Apparently, Sweden and Germany use the IoT which is the 'Internet of Things'. Hahaha, who came up with that name? Was it a menopausal woman? From what my tiny non-tech-savvy brain can work out, this is putting 'software' and 'connectivity' into objects so they can collect, exchange or act on data. Anyway, that's what the AI told me. (I only put 'the' in front of words like AI because it makes my daughters laugh. And laughing at me or with me is fine either way.) These countries are carrying out trials currently, presumably to decide which 'things' they could stuff a load of software into next. How about a packet of biscuits so it could count how many you've had, and if you have more than two in a sitting the packet self-destructs?

There are also trials going on to see how the robot tech being developed gets on with tasks like medication reminders, health monitoring and companionship. Companionship? I'd be happy with the first two being taken on by any old robot you care to name. But companionship? I've got a few friends who are a bit unreliable, but I can't say I've ever wanted to sit with a robot and say, 'Remember when you were just a little pile of metal and wires? Happy days.'

I think this issue is definitely age related. Young people are so much more open to and comfortable with change. Many much younger people have AI counsellors, for example, and seem perfectly happy with them, because they are tech savvy. Or maybe they have lowered their expectations? Although there have been some issues with the robots not quite understanding the job. And why would they? Added to this, one company is using AI-powered robots to do weekly care visits. Is that a terrifying thought? It is for me.

I'm not quite clear how this works either. Firstly, I can't imagine a robot marching down the street towards some poor unsuspecting old person's house and negotiating the dangers that may entail, like dealing with rogue gangs of teenage boys, or standing outside pleading with someone who won't let them in because they're a robot, for God's sake!

Apparently though, these robots don't operate alone (faints with happiness), which must be a bit of a relief to most people. Care robots are being trialled still, so they must have someone with them in case they go a bit haywire, shove you in the bath with your clothes on, make you grass crumble for dinner or defect to a junkyard and convert themselves into a Meccano set that talks.

I think it's fascinating that the sex industry is way ahead in terms of sophisticated robots. No, 'sophisticated' is the wrong word. The phrase I'm looking for is 'sex robots'. It's no surprise that a section of the tech industry, which is almost completely male dominated, has spent more time developing sex dolls with terrifyingly huge bosoms and a willingness to cooperate, rather than considering the needs of elderly people, whose willingness to cooperate can sometimes go on holiday.

So, let's look mainly at 'socially assistive robots' who are designed to combat loneliness and social isolation, whether you want it or not, missus! What do these robots have to offer?

Well, interactive conversations, for a start-off. At least it doesn't just talk at you, which can't be said of some people I know. It will also play games with you, lead exercise routines and provide emotional support. It might be an improvement on some of your relatives.

Given such life-changing developments in technology, there is the inevitable adjustment period to something new and I think that, although young people now will probably be quite comfortable to be looked after by a robot when they are old, it's a big ask for the generation who aren't accustomed to the idea of having high-tech machines looking after them.

These robots are called 'carebots', which hasn't really got a comfortable and homely ring to it, has it? The aim of carebots is to supplement human care, so the carers themselves can focus on more complex issues. (Like what, Fermat's Theorem?) Apparently, the benefits have been shown to be reduced costs and improved well-being for users. (I would imagine reduced costs are the major benefit there for the company.) However, although some people may find them comforting, they're not very 'huggable', are they?

Others think they are not a replacement for human interaction, although the increasing sophistication of AI means that eventually these bots could be indistinguishable from a person. To look at, at least. To be fair, quite a lot of people are indistinguishable from a robot. Although however realistic these machines become there will always be the missing piece of magic which is humanity in all its unpredictable, gory glory. And I presume it would be a huge mistake to build in unpredictability when constructing a carebot, although if you did you could probably have a right laugh with it on holiday.

Let's leave the robots getting ready for their big

moment in the care sector and move back to more familiar territory. There is much modern technology that is an improved version of something people are familiar with and is easier to get used to. A lot of this stuff is now smaller, but much more sophisticated, with the ability to store and use information, which it couldn't do when it was a baby watch, for example. And you can wear it too!

Wearable Tech

Wearable tech is another advance that has revolutionized people's lives and there are many gadgets that you can pop on which will give you a continuous flow of information beneficial to you and anyone looking after your health.

Smartwatches are a very good example. They do so many things other than tell the time. For example, there is a function called 'automatic fall detection', so you know when you've fallen over. All right, sorry, it's so you can have an opportunity to call the emergency services when you've fallen over very heavily. I have a smartwatch which likes to tell me occasionally I've had 'a heavy fall' when I've just got into a car. Love a smartwatch that takes the piss. However, when I really did fall over outside the A&E department – not even a squeak out of my not-so-smart-as-it-thinks-it-is watch. Perhaps I should have waited until it stopped laughing.

Obviously it's great for older people to have a smartwatch, but messaging on it is nigh on impossible for me because my fingers aren't tiny and dextrous, so messages sent from my watch look more like anagrams, such as 'Hepl I flel cown!' I am also constantly being harassed in a comedy way by my daughters for my one-finger technique. Well, at least I'm entertaining them.

Smartwatches can allow you to be tracked if you're an older person who is confused and you wander off and get lost. They can also supply data about heart health, blood pressure, sleep patterns and your menstrual cycle, although that final one ceased to be of use quite some years ago. Of course, with all tech, there are some concerns. First of all, affordability is a big problem because they cost a *lot* of money. Secondly, because they collect sensitive health data, apparently this raises some security concerns. Really? Probably only if you're a very important person like the King or a world leader. I wonder who would be interested in my blood pressure?

So, I think we can agree that, on balance, with all the advances in science and technology, the future of many older people will be improved in many ways with the monitoring of health, home, residential care and safety, but having detailed some of the advances that have been made, I feel moved to ask, 'WHAT ABOUT FUN?'

Surely there are ways that older people's lives can be improved, other than through their health, safety and comfort, to avoid the seemingly inevitable slump into an endless round of same-y days punctuated by grim food and even grimmer entertainment. More fun is what is needed.

What if you could google on your smartwatch 'mobility scooter racing' or 'garages that sell turbo charged rocket shaped vehicles' and you found lots of options – wouldn't that be brilliant? Imagine racing off to the seaside or taking corners on two wheels. But instead, you get pages and pages of adverts for your common-or-garden mobility vehicles. Surely us ageing old harridans deserve a bit of excitement and you and your best friend could do a 'Thelma and Louise' if you so wished (look it up, younger people). Why can't lifelong bikers, who, let's be honest, deserve a bit of excitement in their later years, get something that goes faster than I could walk? I realize I'm creating my own private fantasy of extreme havoc here, but you could also give your favourite bookworm *The History of Mobility Scooters* or programme a vehicle just to visit museums. (Apparently old people like them.) And for those who don't want any excitement at all on their way from A to B, self-drive cars are improving no end and I'd love to see lots of little bright red bubble cars containing old men and women doing their knitting, the crossword, eating crisps or whatever they choose, whilst whizzing around town as their satnav with the voice of Julian Clary guides them on their errands. I can dream.

It's also time for someone to come up with some augmented-reality games for older people. You could play Scrabble against Frank Sinatra or tour round your neighbourhood as it was when you were a child. I'm just making this up as I go along, but if it can be done for teenagers who won't come out of their rooms much, surely it's all wrong that this sort of entertainment can't be provided for people who can't come out of their rooms *at all*? And while AI is getting its act together to offer decent companionship to older people, at least you could be whisked away in your armchair on a virtual-reality cruise. It's just a thought, but in future life could be so much better for older people, if only the tech lot get their act together.

ESSENTIAL EMOJIS

If you have a problem connecting with younger people and you actually care, you could sling a few emojis their way. Here are some useful new ones I made up:

 My hot water bottle needs refilling with vodka.

 Hooray, my bowel cancer test has arrived.

 Fell out of bed.

 No I don't want a fucking Werther's.

 Please don't help me across the road.

 Sorry, can't be arsed.

 My robot carer has arrived.

 I've dismantled my robot carer.

 Unscammable.

 Went too far with the facelift.

 Expecting canvassers.

 Don't send help, it's all under control.

CHAPTER SEVEN

Risky Business

Getting old can be a very risky business. With so many physical, cognitive and emotional changes coming at you, it's hard to process it all. And when you are feeling lonely too, that is when you are least able to see the wood for the trees and may unwittingly lay yourself open to the approach of the scammer – a wily, tech-savvy, amoral little criminal of the first order.

Occasionally I will hear about an older person who has been scammed out of a huge amount of money and think, 'How on earth did he/she fall for that?' But in many ways, it can be understood in the context of the sophistication of the scams, the vulnerability of the scammed person and the unfamiliarity some people may have with how aspects of the modern world operate.

Let's begin with romance scams. The numbers are rising in this country, with a significant increase amongst older age groups. The average loss for 75- to 84-year-olds is £8,000!

If we're honest, romance scams are not normally associated with older people, are they? Occasionally, when you see very sweet pictures in your local paper or online of a couple in a residential home for the elderly, holding hands, you do tend to think 'that's lovely', or 'good on her for nabbing the only bloke in the place', or 'what's my mum doing with that loser? Shit, he must have heard she's got a few quid'. But did you know that 50 per cent of men between the age of 65 and 80 said in a survey they were 'extremely or very interested' in sex? That seems a bit low to me. And what percentage of women said they were 'extremely or very interested' in sex? 'Was it 90 per cent?' I hear you cry.

Sadly not. It was 12 per cent. Even that sounds a bit high to me.

So, it seems that old men are much more interested in sex than old women. Hold the front page! I think the problematic difference between men and women is that women want to believe that a 23-year-old is in love with them, and quite a lot of men, whatever age they are or whatever they look like, *do* believe it. When you see a very old man with a much younger woman (I'm talking thirty years at least), do you think he must be such a nice person, or do you think he's got a wallet the size of his sex drive?

Romance scams among the elderly predominantly take place online on places like Facebook or dating platforms like Tinder. I can just about imagine older people using

Facebook, but Tinder? Surely that's for the *young* people (said the ageist old hag). Its core users are approximately 18–30 years old, and the numbers decline the older you get. So, with a relatively small user group, it's fascinating that older people even get scammed at all and are seemingly much more vulnerable to it. It's possible, I suppose, that older people are able to locate Tinder but not so au fait with the dangers. If I were approached on Tinder by a much younger person, alarm bells would immediately ring, but for some people they don't. As an ex-bellringer, I would be listening out for that loudest of bells. When you're next in central London, stroll past St Paul's Cathedral. Great Paul resides there. No, he's not a bloke everyone loves, but the loudest bell in England, and that's the sort of loud I mean.

But why is this happening?

I've always thought the phrase 'I *want* to believe' sums up a lot of people, and it's difficult because if you are a nice, trusting person, would you really want to end up a cold, hard cynic? (Or maybe you already are one, like me.) Of course, people are much easier to fool online. Yes, yes, especially technophobic old people. Although I think if I received a 'message' from Leonardo di Caprio I'm not sure I would believe that he had really been in touch, making overtures to a 68-year-old. Anyway, I think he likes women fifty years younger than me. But several scams I've heard about have involved a very similar modus operandi to this. This is when I think lonely people are so desperate to believe something so magical has happened that it is somehow easier to silence one's inner voice. My inner voice is the voice of my mum, so I pay *some* attention to it. If I see a picture online of a very elderly woman with a much younger partner, I just assume a scam and/or she's got loads of money and she doesn't care that it's purchased her a young pretender – and good on her for that.

I also wonder whether older people can't quite believe that someone would do that to them, and this propensity for trust is compounded by social isolation, which affects judgement. Perhaps some of them haven't got their glasses on. Maybe they think it'll be fun and then suddenly they're hooked in. Perhaps they don't understand the language of the yoof. As with every generation, old words are commandeered and given new meanings, resulting in a minefield of misunderstandings. Like when I said to one of my daughters when she was a teenager that I was going to 'hook up' with my dad and she fell about laughing. It then of course transpired that this now means 'have sex with'. The word 'moist' was adopted briefly for a while too, apparently, and put to nefarious use, meaning, broadly, 'annoying'. My daughter once said to me, 'Oh God, Mum, you're so moist.' *Not since the menopause*, I thought to myself.

So how do romance scammers do it? Here are some popular ploys to watch out for . . .

Scammers simulate emotional connections and, let's be honest, that is much easier to do through mere words without being able to see a talking head. Also, scammers seem to be very patient and take their time to gain trust – one more reason I'd be useless at it. Another way of extorting your money would be by getting you to share sensitive information and then using it against you. Something like a selfie in your pants, although I would be mighty surprised if someone over the age of 30 has one of these hiding in their phone waiting to be hacked.

And then we come back to vulnerability, with the subheading of loneliness. Loneliness always adds to vulnerability by skewing your judgement and convincing you that because these people approaching you sound lovely, they probably are. And it is often accompanied by its chums Longing and Misplaced Trust. I would also wager that women are far more likely to be people-pleasers and, even though they are reluctant, can't quite bring themselves to say no, as it goes against the grain of how they were brought up. I was brought up this way and have had to take action on a couple of occasions when I was being coerced for money . . . by my daughters.

Early declarations of love are also a trademark tactic. This is blood-out-of-a-stone territory for some women, who see a relationship as a series of hurdles to get over before you get the prize, and so can be a particularly powerful tool wielded by scammers. (Though if you ask me, for a lot of women, after they've sailed over the commitment and marriage hurdles, they find themselves, twenty years down the line, watching TV with a grunting lump and wondering what all the fuss was about.)

And then, of course, scammers assume that older people are unfamiliar with online fraud tactics. This is very true and the whole horrible business can proceed with relatively few barriers, although some find they have relatives to contend with. I have read a lot about these families who see their nearest and dearest being taken in by someone who is quite clearly a charlatan. They feel impotent and angry. Their 85-year-old dad is dating a 25-year-old and the inner cynic shouts that perhaps they've got half an eye on their inheritance too. Often there is very little the family can do, short of crossing their fingers or hiring a hit man.

Many second wives or husbands have felt the icy glare of the previous family, whether they are genuine or not. I was absolutely delighted that neither of my parents found new partners . . . well, not ones they told me about anyway, and ignorance certainly is bliss.

This all points towards a requirement for better education and awareness, but that's so difficult to organize and you'd probably need to do it online, where older people mainly aren't, so maybe we need to come up with new ideas. How about ads in the middle of popular soap operas? Maybe not. Cups of tea will be being made.

I think we need a gameshow!

Cue cheesy upbeat music and an enthusiastic audience cheering. Our host enters from stage left.

Host: Welcome to tonight's *Family versus Gold Digger*!

The curtains open and in comes a young man with a much older woman. Audience reacts accordingly: oohs, aahs and boos.

Host: And now! The Unhappy Family!

A group of three hulking, brutish middle-aged men stumble in.

Host: So, Connor, you're here today with your partner Phyllis.

Connor: That's right.

Host: And you three lads are concerned about your mum?

Lads: That's right.

Host: So, we're bringing on our 'Lover or Liar' detector and that will settle the matter once and for all. Sit in the chair please, Connor . . .

Surely it's not a great stretch to go from *Love Island* to a show which deals with this reasonably common family conflict? And people do love a bit of conflict.

People lose so much money to various scams that they could club together and fund a small country. I suspect it's a hidden shame most of the time, particularly for women who have been fooled by an online romance scam, and even more particularly for older women who feel like they shouldn't even be thinking about *all that nonsense*. There are many things old women are made to feel ashamed of and one of them is a sex life after the age of 60. Well, most old men don't seem to be ashamed of it, and it is up to you to use your old-woman passport to eccentric behaviour to combat it.

Do you know anything about building? I don't and neither would I want to. (And I'm the daughter of a scaffolding designer. So proud.) Many other women are the same. Not because they're women, but because they're just not interested. However, building scams are very popular these days and older people are frequent targets, I'm assuming because they're easier to 'persuade'. Unfortunately, a lot of older people fall for building scams, which includes a lot of older women who live on their own. It seems unlikely that many of them have even heard tell of these scams down the laundrette or in the pub so perhaps it is time to launch one of those educational films like the ones we used to watch at school. Ours were a bit boring and long with no one interesting in them, so I think it needs to be targeted, short, snappy and straight to the point, with only the most important information included. We've all seen those sorts of videos with Professor Somniferous droning on in front of a chalkboard while gentle snoring, or more likely mucking-about, gets going.

So, firstly, you need a presenter favoured by older women. May I suggest Stanley Tucci and bugger the expense? He would outline the issue, maybe do a couple of impressions of cheeky builders at your door and would be dressed as a builder, of course. In fact, he could do a few in a series – *Scamming With the Stars* – and he would make the following points clear:

1. These men just turn up and say they've seen a loose or broken tile on your roof. Well, it's not a group of men it's normally just the good-looking one. (Remember it's all relative with builders.) At this point you should just be saying '*No*' to whoever they are, because anyone who offers you a service at your front door is dodgy from the off, including most local politicians.
2. If they are persistent verging on mildly threatening, just shut the door. If you don't like being rude, say something like, 'My husband is in the bath and I can hear him screaming' before slamming the door.
3. Call the police afterwards if you think it's necessary.
4. Stanley Tucci, or whoever it is that makes the final cut, might also give you a different set of short replies you could try if you're not sure what to say. Something like 'Piss off, you useless numpty.'

5. Stan will also briefly explain the scam to you: they offer to replace a couple of broken tiles and before you know it the roof's off and you owe them £30,000; bish bash bosh, you've been scammed.

And here are some extra suggestions from me to supplement Stanley's brief but informative educational talk:

1. Have a Ring doorbell. This will enable you to get a look at them before you interact with them and you could try what I often do on the phone, which is putting on your best gruff blokey voice. Keep it short in case of squeaks.
2. Keep a very loud recording of a very dangerous-sounding dog and set it off when you don't recognize the caller. Try not to do it if you see the vicar . . . or do if you're a rampant atheist. Alternatively, you could just have a very big fierce dog. Or you could have a small, sweet dog in another part of the house and turn round and shout 'Cerberus!' as you're talking to the scammers.
3. Ask for the registration number of the van and see what happens.
4. Have an ornate Victorian chamber pot with some apple juice in it by the front door. They might just think it's something else and they're

going to get a faceful if they ring the doorbell. Or you could point to it and ask if they want a glass and then be offended when they seem suspicious. This is just a twisted fantasy of mine.

Alternatively, you could do sensible things:

1. Do not answer the door to uninvited traders or at all if you don't like people very much. I'm looking forward to this in a couple of years.
2. Display a 'No cold callers' sticker, even though you might not know what it means, because I don't. (Obviously everyone welcomes a hot caller.)
3. Display a sign saying 'HUGE AGGRESSIVE DOG AND EQUALLY AGGRESSIVE HUSBAND'.
4. Don't pay large sums up front. What am I saying? Don't even engage with them.
5. Or you could try saying, 'Are you *all* my dream Tinder dates come at once?' And watch them leg it.

In many ways, 'scammability' comes down to a few things and I think that those women who attempt to appease others are very near the top of the list. If this is your weak spot, don't even go to the door. Gag yourself with a tea towel and lie on the floor until they've gone.

You might also want to be aware of text messages purporting to be from your children/grandchildren. These tend to be along the lines of, 'Hello Grandma, I'm on holiday in Spain and I've had all my money stolen, please can you send me some or I won't be able to afford an ice cream.' All right, they don't usually say anything like that, but they ask for money normally, and quite a lot of people get fooled by them. If you've never done online banking and you don't know how to do it, keep it that way.

It's understandable that many people might feel they never want to answer the door or pick up the phone again, and if your family can be quite trying, I suppose that's an option.

I should conclude this by saying that technology has become so sophisticated these days and scams so clever that it is advisable not to trust a single unknown caller on any medium. What an appalling state of affairs that is, but if you're suspicious, erring on the side of caution is probably the best approach to take. Unless Tom Allen is at your door telling you that you've won the lottery. He's very trustworthy.

CHAPTER EIGHT
Men: the Clichés

Musings on Old Men

Whenever I think about old men, my thoughts tend to turn to my two grandads, Ted and Ernie. When I was a child, they were really the only two older men I ever had more than fleeting contact with. However, there was one other old man in my life who, although totally benign, looked scary to me as a four-year-old and featured in the odd nightmare from time to time.

This was 'The Rag and Bone Man', who looked ancient, but may only have been 35, it was hard to tell. He was weather-beaten and skeletal and hunched over the reins of a cart drawn by a horse which looked nearly as pissed off as he did. He collected (surprise!) rags and bones for making into paper, glue and soap among other things. Sounds positively Dickensian, doesn't he?

He might not have seemed like it, but he was effectively

an early recycler and, God bless him, looked like he needed recycling too. You could hear him shout, 'Shan't be round tomorrer!' regularly which was everyone's cue to run out and shove a load of empty bottles, old curtains and bones on his cart. And despite 'bones' featuring in his job title, I don't think they were a major part of the donations. And I never got to know his work schedule well enough to know why he wouldn't be round 'tomorrer'.

Other than that, apart from fleeting contact with a vicar here or an ancient farmer there after we moved to the countryside, the only old blokes I tended to see were entering or exiting pubs, although of course I was never able to follow them into these mysterious places. (My 'Following Men into Pubs' era came much later.) And older men rarely encroached on what was almost exclusively the territory of women back then: childcare, housework and all the stuff that women jealously ring-fence for themselves. Hmm.

And that's it for me on the old-man front, which I suppose is indicative to some extent of how little the lives of older men collided with the lives of younger children in the 1950s and 1960s unless they were relatives. Back to my grandads!

When I was a child, the two men were very different from one another, but as they were my only old-man role models for quite a long time, they had to cover every base. For a start, one, Ernie, was very tall, and the other, Ted, was very small. We children therefore renamed them 'Big Grandad' and 'Baby Grandad' and somehow it stuck and everyone in my family started to call them that.

The problem with trying to glean a sense of them both as middle-aged men when I was a child was that firstly, I didn't see either of them nearly as often as I saw my grandmas, because they would both have been at work in the traditional 1950s/1960s roles they fulfilled as the 'men of the house'. They did no childcare whatsoever, so our contact with them was somewhat limited to once every few weeks.

Because of his height, Baby Grandad seemed rather cute, and his face was always settled into a benign expression (the very same expression that my brother Bill always had), whereas Big Grandad was imposing and looked positively brooding at times. However, personality-wise, I'd say a more accurate representation of their characters, according to older relatives, might have been reflected on their faces if they had swapped them over. Because we saw much less of the grandads, they retained a real sense of mystery. In retrospect, they looked very similar to Statler and Waldorf from *The Muppets*.

They did wear very similar clothes, and you could rely on both, come rain or shine, to wear a suit and tie most of the time. 'Leisurewear' hadn't really been invented then (praise the Lord, some might say, including me), so they both made you think they meant business rather than looking like part-time, out-of-shape, elderly athletes in some hideous neon shade.

Baby Grandad had spent a long time in the army and had eventually become a regimental sergeant-major whose bark and bite were much bigger than his height, although from the kick-off he always seemed enormously benign to us, despite apparently being a demon on the parade ground. It's always been a cliché that small men compensate for their lack of height by being fiercer and more dominant. This was known as a Napoleon Complex, and although Baby Grandad was softened somewhat by the prefix of 'Baby' it was certain there were hidden depths, as evidenced by him apparently chasing my dad up the path waving a shotgun the first time he walked my mum home.

Big Grandad had to stay at home during the war because the role of cabinet maker was deemed a 'reserved occupation', which meant these guys were assessed to be more useful at home than away fighting, being on hand in case they were expected to knock up a lovely new drinks cabinet for some toff or other. Let's just say their skills were transferable to other endeavours like producing wooden aircraft components or ammunition boxes. I am very pleased to say, too, that Big Grandad followed the fashion choices of the seaside visitor when on the beach by wearing the legendary knotted hanky on his head, thus upholding the tradition so perfectly portrayed many years down the line in a sketch by the Monty Python gang.

When I think about Baby Grandad, who fought in the Second World War, it makes me think of the poor bastards in the First World War who were scared out of their wits, as any sensible person would be. The narrow choice for them was to stay and possibly get killed, or try and run away and get shot by your own side. Thankfully this barbaric practice was outlawed during the Second World War, but the practice of Not Talking About The War was adhered to by most men afterwards and it is only old soldiers who we ever see weeping when talking about the war, and whose diminishing testosterone has finally allowed them to have a perfectly normal reaction to the trauma of it all.

I know my Baby Grandad met his second wife, my grandma Maisie, when she was a nurse and he was wounded during the war. He was quite a lot older than her, and I think this was frowned upon. His first wife, my mum's mother, had gone off with someone else; it was all very hushed up and not something that was ever really spoken of. Chuck in absolutely no mention of the war on my grandad's part and that's just how it was. Many, many unmentionables.

A friend of my dad, who was quite a bit older than him, was a fighter pilot during the Second World War, and he had been in a bar one night with the rest of his squadron. They all got absolutely off their faces and my dad's friend was so drunk he fell down the stairs that night and broke his ankle. So, the next day, he could not go out on a mission with the rest of his squadron. They went without him and not one of them came back. This is just one example of the weirdness of fate and something some people would never get over. It's hard to know to what degree feelings are suppressed after calamitous events like this, and whether the generation of young guys, for whom nothing like counselling or anti-depressants were available, passed on their trauma. Looking at this guy in my dad's sitting room, you couldn't meet a more placid, sweet-tempered man and wouldn't have imagined for a minute any of the stuff he'd been through.

For a long time throughout history, men weren't really permitted by society to show their emotions in any meaningful way, because it wasn't *manly*. They were supposed to be 'strong and silent'. In those days, if you couldn't really tell what was going on with a man, he was doing the right thing as far as society was concerned. Phrases like 'grin and bear it' were liberally sprinkled around, feelings were disguised and men were looked down upon if they dared to say they felt unhappy or anxious.

In those days, and I am not basing it on a very representative sample, as I didn't make a habit of hanging out with many old men when I was a child, but men's habits and activities seemed very separate from women's. After he retired, Big Grandad seemed to be either at the bookies or in front of the telly with a paper and a bookie's pen behind his ear and, although Baby Grandad died relatively young from cancer, I do remember he spent a lot of time doing that 'pottering about' thing.

As young kids, Baby Grandad used to tell us, when we asked why his teeth were kept in a glass overnight, that the teeth would cut the lawn for him when everyone was in bed, and that image has stayed in the back of my mind ever since. His was certainly one of the most manicured lawns I've ever come across!

The social prism of 'chivalry', for want of a better word – and I don't mean knights defending a maiden's honour and all that stuff, but the day-to-day thing of holding doors open, tipping your hat at the ladies, and paying for everything – went hand in hand with the designation of 'Head of the Household', 'Manager of Finances' and 'Driver of the Car'. I, for one, am glad all that 'little woman' crap is no longer with us and the presumption of weakness that goes with it. (I am excluding giving old women and pregnant women a seat on the bus here, obviously.) I seem to remember Big Grandad doing quite a lot of shepherding of my grandma through doors, into cars and along pavements. I don't remember it seeming proprietorial at the time and even if it did, I certainly didn't know big words like that back then.

I remember that lots of men used to go to football and if you look at footage of matches back then when my grandads were young, everyone was dressed exactly the same: coats, caps and club scarves. The matches were attended almost exclusively by men, unless, I presume, you were the wife of someone important. When their team scored, everyone seemed obliged to throw their caps in the air, which probably meant that a lot of caps landed back on the wrong owner and many men came home with someone else's cap. This didn't matter though, because they were Head of the Family, so their wife could not tell them off.

Depending on which team you supported, watching football would have been an enjoyable pastime near to your home and you could go down to the ground with your mates (exclusively male) and watch at a relatively reasonable price. (This is unfortunately not the case these days if you support a premier league club, as many loyal fans are being priced out of the market.)

In those days, a lot of women didn't really know or want to know or weren't allowed to know anything about football. I remember doing a joke about men thinking women footballers put the ball in their handbag and got their husbands to give them a lift to the goal. That attitude has changed pretty much beyond recognition, given the stellar re-emergence of the women's game, which rose again from the ashes of being banned by the FA in 1921 due to 'health concerns', when in fact they were worried about the women's game overshadowing the men's because it was drawing such big crowds, having got a foothold during the First World War. So, one can only hope that the current generation of girls will also be glued to matches when they're old too, should they want to be!

We never played football at school and were fed a diet of netball, rounders and hockey: games for LADIES. Hockey was a bit grim. I always played in goal. Not very demanding, but freezing cold, boring and hard work being dressed as an American ice-hockey player. Both my brothers loved playing and following football. Being the middle child, and a girl, who knew very little about football, I had a team chosen for me and that team was West Ham, who I still retain a soft spot for. It was also an opportunity for my brothers to give me a mild kicking or relentlessly tease me if they lost, and I was very easy to wind up in those days. It seems to be a lottery as a young child that you pick a team which isn't necessarily down the road from you, but one that has your favourite famous players in it. We were in Kent, but both my brothers plumped for Manchester United players because they were so much more glamorous. My brothers loved George Best and Bobby Charlton. On such flimsy premises are our loyalties constructed as children.

Incidentally, I met Bobby Charlton quite a few years ago and what a lovely man he was. My brother Matt was in the very late stages of cancer and Sir Bobby wrote him a message on a programme, which I know he loved. Bobby Charlton spent his last few years in a nursing home where he died in 2023. This absolute hero, who survived the

Munich air disaster, being pulled from the wreckage by the goalkeeper, ended his days after falling and breaking a bone in a nursing home, which is a timely reminder of the democracy of old age. The privilege for me of meeting such a legend and being able to do something like that for my brother was brilliant.

I would imagine being expected to be the strong silent type in public must have been quite stressful for men of my grandads' era. And I'm sure that wives saw a very different side to husbands who were struggling to present a manly face to the world. Obviously, it was impossible as a little girl to know what was going on with my grandads as we only saw the grandad face they put on for my brothers and me. There was just an aura of all-round benign manliness, and we were one of those families that rarely made emotional displays of any kind, especially when the grandparents were around.

Quite a few people seem to think the disappearing phenomenon of 'manliness' has gone too far and there is too much open expression of 'feelings' by young men these days. I occasionally hear people say, 'How would they get on if they had to go to war?' On the other hand, there is a sizeable group of young men who are frustrated by the power they see many women appearing to have. These are the residents of the Manosphere and unfortunately for them their hero has not turned out to be much of a hero.

Quite a lot of older people think young people are too

soft these days; I wouldn't care to judge. Children crying 'excessively' used to be very much frowned upon when we were kids and the phrase 'Be quiet or I'll really give you something to cry about' gives you a clue as to how emotional expression was not encouraged for boys or girls. Corporal punishment and smacking have now largely been replaced these days with 'gentle parenting', and for some this 'abomination' needs to be stopped before society completely falls apart. I think an educationalist who comes up with a way to put the brakes on increasingly uncontrolled behaviour in schools will probably get the Nobel Peace Prize.

So how is the future looking for male ageing?

How men behave now will have a huge bearing on what sort of old men they become, and given the advance of technology and monumental changes to people's lives in a relatively short time, it's fascinating to think forward to what young people's experiences of old age will be like in generations to come. Apparently, a biomedical gerontologist (whatever that is) has predicted that one day ageing could be 'cured' through medical advances and will be a treatable 'condition' by 2050. This guy was fired from a research foundation he co-founded in 2021 after an independent investigation concluded he'd made offensive remarks to two women. So perhaps he qualifies as a dirty old man, although he looks more like a body double for Albus Dumbledore. But let's put Albus to one side for now and look at how Gen Z men will fare as they age.

Apparently, Gen Z men are far more concerned with their appearance than past generations of men and seem to be using products that used to be almost exclusively the domain of women. So, no longer the rugged, weather-beaten look of the adventurer, or the trousers-up-to-the-chest braces wearers, who run a cursory flannel over their faces and hope for the best. Nowadays serums and lotions are being liberally slapped on to enable men to head towards the Peter Pan stable. Gen Z are also using speciality shampoos and conditioners for thinning hair. Maybe someone should tell them that nearly 90 per cent of women regard bald men as more confident and masculine.

Apparently, Gen Zs are going to redefine old age through having something called 'micro-retirements', which apparently means regular, planned career breaks. I wonder if they'll let the boss know? They'll be expected to adopt unconventional career paths because they favour 'purpose over stability'. Purpose over stability was not readily available as a choice when my father's generation was young. Many men did the same job for most of their lives and got a carriage clock at the end if they were lucky, retiring on the dot at the time they were supposed to, to take up a hobby known as 'trying not to get under their wives' feet at home'. Medicine was in a very different place then and there wasn't really a longevity button you could press, men just had to hope they had inherited decent genes. Gen Zs, financially speaking, will need to work for longer. And given that the number of centenarians is ever-expanding and a lot of people who retire are very bored doing nothing, it seems like a great idea.

The social lives of Gen Zs will be, as they are now, heavily integrated with technology, unless the dinosaurs get their act together and take over. I'm not sure about the prospect of sitting in the same spot for the next twenty to thirty years with technology offering you communication, shopping options and onscreen socializing – it sounds like the motivation to move will diminish and, who knows, in the future we may have a new breed of human: 'half-man-half-armchair'. So, Gen Zs will be 'hyper-digital seniors', which regretfully is the polar opposite of me as I am a hyper-Luddite senior. I do not like that 'senior' word much. The constant euphemistic language is rather wearing, don't you think? Why not just call old people 'brilliant old superhumans who are never knowingly less than fascinating and a right laugh'.

Gen Zs will also be focusing on digital health. Well, I suppose you need to have healthy fingers to use those laptops. In fact, they'll be healthier generally as they have eschewed smoking and drinking, so they might be quite miserable, and having stuffed themselves with UPFs there's a danger this will have a damaging counter-effect on all their health gained from stopping smoking and drinking, so they'll be just like us.

It seems that millennial men these days are much more enthusiastic than they used to be about stepping across the long-drawn line in bold separating the roles of parents which years ago were very clearly delineated. No longer does the man go to work while his wife stays at home with a duster. These days both partners need to work to make the financial side of having a child work, and play an exhausting game of childcare tag with the help of nearby relatives, nursery and friends, and often that burden is falling on the lucky grandparents. Plus, the provisions for children that are struggling with previously undiagnosed conditions such as ASD are going to add an extra burden. Is anyone going to be able to manage any hobby other than lying down and groaning?! (Though that does have some benefits as a very relaxing hobby.) When you factor in all the above, perhaps it's not surprising that the birth-rate is falling at a slightly alarming rate, and many couples have dispensed with the idea of having any children at all.

It is, I think, a major step in the right direction that increasingly, for many parents, rearing children is an equal venture with their partner, so that everyone has the same amount of time for leisure, whether that's dropping unconscious into bed for a few hours (better than holding a Tupperware party like they did in the sixties) or heading off on a golf weekend (or something not quite so innocuous). (Incidentally, and sorry to sound like a grumpy old woman, but everything leisurely these days goes on so much longer than it used to. For example, stag and hen nights became weekends or moved up to whole weeks and I presume will eventually extend to such great lengths of time that there will be no point coming back to get married at all. Although weddings now seem to have extended into weeks in some far-flung location anyway. End of rant.)

So, as traditional roles have blurred more, each generation seems to have some sort of unforeseen burden to carry. We may discover in the next generation that societally things change so much that the running of a household is taken over by robots, as robot hoovers clean the house, drones deliver the shopping and the post, self-drive cars may be programmed to drive the kids to school, robot pets will walk themselves and all you'll need to do is think or watch sport. Looking good for all you old guys!

CHAPTER NINE
Men v. Women

All this talk of men has got me pondering. Who lives longer, men or women? And does it really matter?

To some extent, doing a head count in a residential home for the elderly will give us a good idea of who's winning the gendered staying-alive game of chance, and it certainly seems to be women.

I know I'm making this sound like a competition, and that's my fault, because I've always been like this. My mum was a full-on feminist, so much of society was reframed by her as the 'battle of the sexes', and every small victory made a difference. I know men are ahead of women in so many areas of society like pay, top jobs and politics, so is living a few years longer than them anything to write home about? The answer is probably no, but the reasons are interesting, because I think they say so much about the sort of society we were and how that is changing into something very different.

I'm sure a lot of us are very aware of just how rigid the British upper lip has been for many, many years and how that appears to be changing these days, morphing into something positively trembly and jelly-like now men in particular are, thankfully, *finally* permitted to have some feelings they can openly express in a way that was previously forbidden. This constant repression must have caused a shedload of emotional problems further down the line.

Let's look at an area I've always been fascinated by. This is the utterly bizarre phenomenon of men refusing to seek medical help until things have become critical, if not unsalvageable.

Now, I'm not saying it's all men; it's not. In fact, let's use an infuriating acronym 'NAMALT' or, 'Not All Men Are Like That', which is a common response on various online forums, mainly to feminists 'moaning' about male behaviour.

So, trading like for like, I would reply, 'BALOTA' – 'But A Lot Of Them Are'.

And then, of course, back comes 'WAYSAROF' – 'Why Are You Such A Ridiculous Old Feminist?'

To which I reply, 'TOYBAPHDOYMOMA' – 'Take Off Your Blinkers And Put His Dinner On You Moody Old Man Apologist'.

To which they reply, 'SWBAMNPIWOATMAWAD-AWWAND' – 'Society Would Be A Much Nicer Place If

Women Only Accepted That Men And Women Are Different And Women Wore A Nice Dress'.

To which I reply, 'STFU.' (I think we all know what that means.)

Anyway, we could talk nonsense like this until the end of time but obviously none of us have got until the end of time. Well, Bryan Johnson might have if he sticks to his guns.

I have heard a couple of older men say that, as children, it was communicated to them that it was somehow unacceptable to express any kind of emotion openly in response to a difficult issue, be it pain or upset of any kind. ('Big boys don't cry', was a common one.) And so with many men, this morphed into a refusal to seek medical or psychological help until it was unavoidable.

This extreme reluctance to seek help does seem to apply mainly to the 'it's only a flesh wound' generation, who will say this sort of thing as every conceivable organ is emptying itself out through one of their orifices. I get the impression that these men didn't really talk to each other about their mental health either. This seemed to be part of a code that most males were aware of and if you expressed any feelings that weren't 'manly' you would be considered less of 'a man'. This was entirely a social construct, and this message has recently, thankfully, morphed into one that is much more concerned with well-being than putting on some sort of big brave front.

I must confess that I do like to watch the odd 'Ambulance' type show and from experience it seems to me that there is a case to be made for men not being brave at all but being shit-scared like the rest of us and equally susceptible to pain, instead of not doing anything about it until the very last minute. Recently, I've heard one ad campaign on the radio which attempts to encourage men, particularly black men, to test for prostate cancer. They are twice as likely as white men to end up getting prostate cancer, so it is even more essential for them to do this.

It's hard, I suppose, to convince people that the first option of early detection is so much better than the second (doing nothing), and that ignoring things and keeping your fingers crossed isn't very effective.

In the 1950s, when I was born, medicine wasn't nearly as advanced as it is now, but as time goes on, the better the chances are of longevity for both sexes equally. It is true that the longevity gap between men and women is getting narrower. I must admit that, overall, I'd just assumed women were generally 'fitter' – not in terms of describing an attractive woman, or being very good at the long jump, but more in a tortoise and a hare way. So, let's just imagine that women have plodded evenly through life and passed a fair few exhausted men on the way. But is longevity the be all and end all for humanity? I think *quality* of life has been sacrificed for length and that's a difficult thing to tackle without sounding like a moral judgy type or Mrs Cliché.

Let's kick off with the advantages a male or female baby might have before he or she is even born. So, two parents with good genes, no inherited illnesses or propensity for any life-limiting diseases further down the line is always good.

Already, though, before they are born, women have an advantage because they possess two X chromosomes. This gives them a genetic advantage which men do not have. That's as far as I'm going into the genetic side of things as I'm not a geneticist, in case you hadn't realized.

I would guess if we were trying to come up with an image of the average person who probably lives the longest it would be a wealthy woman who exercises regularly, eats well, doesn't smoke, doesn't sunbathe, does nothing to excess and is very, very boring. Well, I wouldn't get on with her.

I studied evolution as part of my degree and most of it was centred on Charles Darwin, the godfather of evolutionary theory, and I used to secretly nurse a wish that Charles Darwin's theory 'survival of the fittest' was in fact a misprint and should have been survival of the 'fattest'. But, let's be honest, how often do fat people get a break? I think we all know the answer to that.

Looking at the major illnesses that we are all at risk from, it seems that cancer is *the* main one, and one that, as I mentioned, men are failing to test for far enough in advance. Men are 40 per cent more likely to die of it than women. That's a yawning gap, isn't it?

Women, on the other hand, do tend to be pretty good about responding to requests for tests. For the lady areas of the body, that is. I have been to every single test or dutifully carried out the ones that have been sent to me. OK, it's not always going to be good news, but it's better than the alternative. And women have to have a huge number of tests throughout their lives. Excuse me while I just run through my favourites pain-wise, ranked from least painful to absolutely bloody agonizing.

Bowel Cancer Test

This comes in a little parcel with a tiny little scoop and a tiny little bottle, so at least you can organize it in the privacy of your own home instead of in a medical arena with seventeen medical students and a suitable soundtrack. It's up to you how you tackle the pooing bit. The test is somewhat fiddly and a bit undignified, but you'll work it out. **Indignity: 1/10. Pain: 0/10.**

Lung Scan

I went to a big mobile caravan thing in Sainsbury's car park after a grilling on the phone. It was very efficient, involved lying down in a scanner and was over in seconds. **Indignity: 2/10. Pain: 0/10.**

(There was a tiny bit of indignity for me only because there was a bit of 'Haven't I seen you on the telly?' Not what you want to hear when you know that at some point they might not be delivering you the best news!)

Breast Screening

Not pleasant. Squashed and flattened on two parallel panels. (Not all of you, just the relevant bits.) The bigger or smaller your protuberances are, the more it's likely to hurt. **Indignity: 5/10. Pain: 5/10.**

Cervical Smear

All I'll say is brace yourselves, but don't wimp out, it's *really* important.

I think women also find it easier to talk to each other about health issues and exchange information about various tests, so apologies if I'm teaching my grandmother to suck eggs (which I can't say I've ever tried myself). I suppose it won't be until men are more comfortable about it that things will really change. I fear much older men are perhaps already a bit of a lost cause, but that's no reason to stop having a go at them about it.

These days there are many groups catering to the various aspects of men's lives centred around health and social concerns that they would never have dreamed of expressing out loud in my day. So perhaps one day stag weekends will be all chats and coffee (*laughs out loud*). Having said that, hen weekends seem to have become an orgy of alcohol and abandon, so I don't know what I'm talking about. I always thought the huge difference between hens and stags was that men would go and see strippers for serious reasons and women would go and see male strippers for a laugh. (Though this isn't always the case. I found myself in a pub on the Old Kent Road many years ago with a friend, and a male stripper at the older end of middle-age appeared at our table dressed as Batman. The only word I can apply to the experience is 'excruciating'. He ended up somehow sitting half on my friend's shoulders and trying to cover both him and her with his cloak. We moved faster than lightning when she realized he wasn't actually wearing anything on his bottom half. 'Did you complain?' No, we ran as fast as we could.)

Where were we? Oh yes – consulting a doctor early on is something men do need to be doing more of, not to mention taking advantage of all the tests that come their way, some of which they can do in the privacy of their own home.

Another big issue affecting the differential death rates

between men and women is that men take far more risks than women, which I think includes driving too fast for a start. You only have to cast your eyes over the totally laddish show *Top Gear* and it will be quite apparent in that particular milieu, given the number of lucky escapes they've all had, just how close to the edge of very serious injury or worse they have come. That's not to say women aren't moving towards more risky pursuits, because they are. I have to confess I wimped out of 'Star in a Reasonably Priced Car' on *Top Gear* because I am so competitive that I did wonder if I'd take far too many risks. Same goes for *The World's Most Dangerous Roads*. No thank you, missus! (By the way, I can't believe I'm saying this, after doing some training as a rally driver, getting my international licence and nearly going off a cliff. A story for another day.)

It seems, however, that scientists might finally have established the reason why females have a better life expectancy than males in the animal kingdom. In order to attract mates (sexual partners, not friends), the males have developed certain traits which result in extra features, like antlers or manes, not to mention using up energy fighting other males. The fighting tends to be quite risky when you're up against another lion, for example, and this can result in injury and maybe early death. However, monogamous species are different, facing far fewer dangers. It seems to be the case that it is the care-giving sex that often lives longer. So, what does that say to you? 'Is it that Jeremy Clarkson and team are going to grow antlers?' I hear you cry, because they are doing the risk-taking equivalent in male human form. Sadly not, though I'd love that. But the message comes across loud and clear that care-givers live longer in an evolutionary sense. Let's all look forward to the *Top Gear* crèche, shall we?

I've often thought about how the division of labour within a marriage will probably predict how well one half of a couple will cope on their own with the practical tasks. Within the older generation, relationships between men and women are probably a more bit traditional in a Theresa May style. She was prime minister from 2016 to 2019 and caused some controversy in an interview when she stated that she and her husband split the household tasks into 'girl jobs' and 'boy jobs'. There was something of an uproar in response, but girl jobs and boy jobs existed for generations, and I suspect in some families they still do. I for one don't have a bloody clue where the stop cock is. Added to this, I hate cooking and I can't stand baking (terrible admission for someone who presents a baking show). My husband, however, is a very good cook and baker, whereas I genuinely do prefer the more mindless housework-type tasks precisely because they are mindless. If I ever find myself separated from my husband and starving hungry, at least I can be proud that my cutlery drawer is the fifteenth tidiest in our street.

My mum did do all the cooking when I was a kid, but I could tell she didn't really like it, because looking back she rotated four or five easy-ish meals and her baking extended to crumbles and rock cakes. Absolutely fine by us children, it's more than a lot of people have, and I have unwittingly followed suit. I cannot remember my dad ever doing anything resembling cooking, baking or housework. Then when he split up with my mum, I think he had to improvise and thanked the Lord when ready meals appeared on the scene. He also discovered the joys of kebabs quite late on in life.

Of course, the issue is, what happens if you're on your own and something technical goes wrong? I have discovered the joys of online technical tutorials on almost everything, particularly simple things that most people under the age of 100 would automatically know. So, for example, I recently watched a video on how to change the battery on my phone and thought it was hilarious when a message on screen came up saying, 'This is for entertainment purposes only.'

Women tend to be more sociable, especially as they age, so would probably cope better on their own, and old men are less likely to ask for help, which kind of makes for a double whammy of trouble ahead.

I think male sociability tends to be linked to a specific activity in the older generation: the football gang, the pub lot, etc. Women traditionally glued the family network together, but we mustn't forget that many families fall out and so how an older person will cope on their own is down very much to their social circle and mobility in terms of how isolated they might be. So, in other words, try not to completely fall out with your kids, or alternatively, start being really nice to them again at a critical stage, although I advise never going to sleep on an argument. At least, stay up and bellow at each other until it's sorted or you've lost your voice. I made things up with my dad eventually after I'd received a big cheque from him. Only kidding. It's important. Life's too short, as they say, as am I.

Of course, the social reach of a family will govern whether they will be able to rally round and cope if an older family member is left alone. Years ago, extended families tended to stay in roughly the same area, and whereas children of the family would be near enough to offer some care, the next stage involved them moving further away and having their own families. These days, many under-25s live a global life far from the country in which their parents are, and having a handy spinster in the family with no hobbies just round the corner who can immediately step in and take up the reins care-wise is increasingly unlikely. If both my daughters had expressed a wish to work at a research facility in the Antarctic, I would always have wondered.

DATING

The rising anxiety at the thought of getting intimate with another human you may only just have met (get your *Knitting Weekly* out, Grandmama, if you just expostulated, Enid Blyton style, with righteous horror) tends to increase as you age. Although I am not denying the hideous anxiety that all ages can suffer when trying to make a snap assessment of how they look to the potential partner, which only multiplies as more layers come off.

That's why in the olden days many encounters took place in the dark, and it's a useful thing to remember that unless you are wearing your 'Most Attractive Person in the World' award, we all have hidden anxieties about how we appear to the other person. I actually think I look all right with very few clothes on (cue explosive guffaw from me), but I know people who are really beautiful who think they look like a pasty little piglet that nobody could possibly fancy, so confidence isn't necessarily related to looks.

The older you get, and as you start to see all the little blemishes expand to link up across your areas, the more this anxiety tends to increase. Perhaps even more so if you've only ever had the one, or very few, sexual partners. This continuum runs from keeping your coat on to swinging with abandon from the nearest equivalent to a chandelier.

Looking at the dating websites for older people they do all seem a bit samey. All the photos are of attractive 'mature' people dressed in neutral colours and looking, well, sensible. This is one of the parts of ageing that's difficult for some older people, because to society it's easy just to become an indistinguishable blob. These dating websites tend to feature younger, better-looking people, and the women always look younger than the men, but that's women's currency. Pity I didn't get that memo.

Hopefully in the future, when we've proved beyond all doubt that quite a lot of us can live a very long time, the dating apps will improve. I would like to see a few varied dating websites that accommodate all different kinds of women, so everyone can feel at home somewhere should they chose to get on the apps:

'Rough as old boots!'

We offer you the chance to *not* make the effort, relax, let what hair you've got left down and meet people in an environment that doesn't scream, 'Oh dear, she's let herself go.' If you like attractively dressed women who are friendly but reserved, piss off elsewhere. But if you need new glasses, come along and have a laugh with us. You don't even have to be looking for love. In fact, if you are and you've had a shower in the last twenty-four hours, why not try our sister organization:

'Lady-I-like'

If demure is your thing, come along and meet women who like a bit of baking, a bit of sewing, a bit of knitting, a lot of housework and making a nice cup of tea - for you! But what they like most of all is running round after you and letting you do whatever you want, whenever you want to. Does your house smell like a drain? Fear not, our ladies will have it smelling of roses in no time, not to mention buying you some new pants and encouraging you to go to the pub and the footie.

Fantasy fun lads?

Looking for a much younger woman to share some intimate moments with? Got a lot of money? No? Well, piss off then.

And now some for the men, so they don't feel left out:

Mr get-your-headphones-in

Ladies! This man is beautifully dressed, good-looking and, God, what a bore. But don't worry, you can just gaze in wonder at him, whilst listening to a feminist rant from your favourite feminist. Enjoy the view.

Man-o-sphere

We all love a rosy-cheeked jolly gentleman to bounce off, so here's your opportunity! Cuddly, bubbly and fun. Give him a spin!

Nice 'n' normal

Not looking for Prince Charming or Albert Einstein? Tired of the sports bores? Just want to meet someone who's a good laugh and fun to be with? Well, join up to NNN. Have a picnic, watch a film, grout the bathroom, see where it goes. Friends with benefits? Friends on benefits? The choice is yours.

CHAPTER TEN

Stop Moaning and Eat Your Sandwich

Have you ever looked around and thought, 'Hmm, people do seem to be eating a lot of sandwiches these days'? I actually have, but this is nothing to do with the term the 'sandwich generation', which, simply put, refers to a generation of (mainly) women who are in a position where they care not only for their own children but are supporting their parents as well. Of course, there are quite a few variations. For example, if you have one or more of your own adult kids living nearby, or at home still owing to financial constraints, and one of them also has a small child who you are helping with, whilst still caring for one or two elderly parents, then you are part of a smaller 'club sandwich generation'. And if you also have an elderly grandparent who needs some sort of care, you are, well, stuffed. The 'stuffed club sandwich generation'. Suffice to say, you are probably female, exhausted, stressed and a very skilful juggler, in case you feel like running away to the circus.

There are so many reasons this situation has arisen, so let's start with money, because it figures in many if not most of the reasons that lives are turned upside down, requiring the poor old piggy-in-the-middle to step up. Firstly, rising costs mean that children are having to live at home for much longer as they can't afford to move out. I moved out when I was 17 by the kind invitation of my mum and dad, who simply couldn't put up with me any longer. Looking back, I don't blame them. I was awful. Never where I said I was going to be (like school), a boyfriend who was every parent's worst nightmare, friends they couldn't bear, *and* I *never* tidied my bedroom. At the time I felt justified because they had moved me from a school I loved to one I couldn't stand but, looking back, I'm not sure that was a good enough reason at all. Anyway, I was delighted to get out of home but definitely could not afford it these days if I was 17, and it seems neither can many people under the age of 30.

Many school-leavers are forced, if they go to university at all, to continue to live with their parents. Many of them are lucky to get a job, let alone one which pays them properly, so even if they wanted to leave home they couldn't. Added to that there are so many more younger people who could not cope with living independently and have poor mental health and/or behavioural problems – an added stress for their parents. Children of a certain age are struggling more too, especially the ones who finished their school education during the Covid era and have struggled to slot themselves quite so easily into the world of work.

In addition, if you had children young, you may find yourself becoming a grandparent in your mid-forties and being called upon to look after your grandchildren regularly as there are not enough nursery places unless they were signed up the second those two blue lines were spotted on the pregnancy test. It's almost like there's no escape these days whatever age you decide to have your children at.

At the other end of Spectrum Sandwich are older people living much longer with all the attendant health problems that go with that, and for which they will need practical support, like having someone to go to appointments with. Older people are also accruing years of increasing additional care needs as more diagnoses are added to their list and they become more frail. Quality of life seems to come a poor second to longevity in this day and age. The ability to keep people living for longer and longer, whatever the circumstances, increases the pressure on those around them who care for them, some of whom may be struggling to do so while also trying to hold together a home and possibly more than one job.

And if things are difficult for any of your older parents living alone, the options, apart from moving them in with you, are finding some appropriate level of care for them to take the pressure off you a bit. Your options, depending on how worried you are about your parent, range from technology for alerting others about specific issues, for example if your relative tends to fall a lot, to employing regular carers. Cash registers pinging merrily! These bits of kit are rather prosaically named 'fall alarms'. They alert a care service who go round and check. If your relative lives miles away I would imagine there is always a side dish of anxiety as you go about your day waiting for the next piece of news about your elderly parent.

The not-being-able-to/not-wanting-to look after your loved ones has morphed into a squillion-pound business these days, as there are now so many professional carers available through private companies. I can just imagine the conversation:

> Company representative: Hello, madam, I understand you are considering live-in care for your mother at home?
>
> Daughter: Yes, please, could you give me an approximate number for how much a year it might cost?
>
> Representative: Yes, that would be around £95,000.
>
> Daughter: (*gulps*) Could you just do the first three days?
>
> Representative: Of each week?
>
> Daughter: No, of just the first week, please.

Representative leaves very quickly. Daughter picks up mobile and makes a call.

Daughter: Doug, could you start clearing your exercise stuff and *Star Wars* collection out of the spare room? Why? I'll tell you later, dear.

A friend of mine worked for a care company visiting people in their homes. Some days she would have as many as seventeen(!) visits on her list. Unfortunately, she didn't have a TARDIS, which meant she had to travel between clients in a mere Earth-bound car, which as you can imagine left her severely restricted as to what she could do in the forty-one seconds she managed to have at each person's house. All right, it wasn't that bad, but she could only do the bare minimum and said she'd have liked to chat for a bit, but it simply wasn't practical.

Times have changed too, in the sense that these days, both parents in a family are obliged to work, whereas before, tradition dictated that the woman of the family would stay at home, bring up the children and take responsibility for any older relatives that weren't coping alone at home. This may be the case for some still, but in an age when people need to have lots of different jobs to survive, or even just pay the electricity bill, many simply cannot offer the care necessary.

Not only are care homes exorbitantly priced, but some people may think twice about placing an older person there because they have heard stories of poor care and treatment. Concerned relatives have been known to install hidden cameras in an elderly person's room so they can check their relative is not being physically or emotionally abused by carers in any way – a grim thought. One issue with closed institutions, big or small, is that once a dangerous milieu is established by the person in charge, it is hard to be the one who blows the whistle. Nobody seems to thank you for it, and I find that so odd, because, in theory, calling out abuse of any kind should be a positive thing.

So, it is an infernal, tortuous mix for the parents in the middle of the sandwich who were looking forward to a bit of peace and quiet. Some hope!

Added to that, these days, many women are delaying having children until later in life for all manner of reasons, including wanting to prioritize their careers, waiting until they have financial stability, or perhaps it just took them a very long time to find a nice partner. Classic sandwich combo of their parents' care needs overlapping with caring for their own children.

I found myself in the position of having children in my mid-forties, so I ended up as a parent/grandparent combo in other people's eyes, and I would often wander half-dead from sleep deprivation through the park, bleary-eyed and clutching a double espresso, to be told what lovely grandchildren I had. It happened so often

I just ended up saying, 'Thanks, so much,' in a quavery voice to avoid further conversation. If I had a pound for every time someone said, 'What lovely grandchildren!' to me, I'd probably have about seventy quid.

My mum had me and my brothers when she was half the age I was when I had my daughters. That's quite a big gap, isn't it? Not only age-wise but energy-wise as well. Looking back, I seem to remember I almost segued directly from the sleepless nights of small children into perimenopause. Lucky me. In fact, if the menopause happens when your children are teenagers that's like having a constant rubbish firework display in your house for the next few years.

So, to summarize, theoretically you could find yourself with a parent living with you who cannot cope in their own home, a child in their twenties still living with you too, not to mention having to find some time to look after your other grown-up children's kids. It sounds absolutely exhausting, doesn't it?

This then is how we arrived at the so-called 'sandwich generation'. It could just as easily be in reference to the fact that a sandwich is also about all you'll get to eat whilst driving from one place to another, or manically running around, as a lunch break is about as likely as Harry Styles asking you out for dinner.

Many moons ago, families all tended to live near each other in the same community, so even if they all hated each other's guts, there was very little most people could do about it. People probably ended up having to look after elderly relatives they couldn't stand, alongside caring for their own children, who hopefully they could stand. But since the law stating it was all right for women to say they are pissed off came into existence, things have started to change, and you don't have to be a martyr any more unless you really want to.

Obviously, in those days, few people tended to live to a very old age, so close family weren't having to minister to the needs of a lovely or possibly cantankerous relative for quite so long. However, the number of people living to a hundred has doubled in the last twenty years and, one could imagine, a bad-tempered, unpleasant relative is going to wear you down eventually.

I realize this is a tricky area, but not all carers are angels all of the time. Hold the front page! I am sure Florence Nightingale and many other heroines of nursing, fondly remembered for their superhuman ability to dedicate their lives to caring for others, had their off-days. I always found it hilarious in comedies about hospitals in my day how matrons and their ilk were always portrayed as bitter and vindictive, implying that a life spent in ministering to the needs of others turns you into some sort of literally monstrous cliché.

Weirdly, I was once asked to audition for a film to play a matron in a residential home for older people. Not sure why because I am not a good actor. I was, however, entranced by the description of the character in the script as 'fat and hideously ugly'. Blimey, I thought, make-up and prosthetics are going to have to work *really* hard.

I didn't go for it in the end and never got to see or hear anything about the film and who the hideously ugly fat person was. Conversely, I did audition for a Harry Potter film to play an inflated aunt who floats up in the air and explodes. I went to the audition just out of curiosity at a studio just outside the M25 and took my daughter, who was really young at the time. It was atmospherically appropriate as there was very thick fog. The two women working on reception were delighted to see a baby and immediately volunteered to look after her. The director asked me to read the script *eleven* times and I thought, 'I'm well in here!' Wrong! It went to the fantastic Pam Ferris, who I think is wonderful and a proper actor, unlike me. I am not being self-deprecating here. I once got a review saying, 'Everyone was overacting apart from Jo Brand who can't act at all.'

Women have always been the main carers since the beginning of time and have learned how to just get on with it because they really had no choice whatsoever. I admire the mavericks through the centuries, like Amelia Earhart, Rosa Parks and Marie Curie, and increasingly since the 1900s, far more women's voices have been heard, thanks to a bunch of women chaining themselves to railings to get the vote (nightmare if you'd left your crack pipe in the car) or chucking flour around at the Miss World competition (better than baking with it, in my opinion), so that finally women are able to see what some other alternatives might be. I'm not suggesting men take over all the domestic caring roles completely, and I know some men occasionally pick up a tea towel, but it would be great to have completely equal choice. To this end many women are now opting to by-pass having a child in favour of having a dog. I see many dogs around these days who have better clothes on than my children ever had.

I did ask AI what to do if unable to cope with looking after an older relative as well as children or grandchildren, and although I assume it tried its best, it came out with the same old waffle about getting regular breaks, having counselling, etc., etc. I'm convinced that if the assumption was that mainly men would be doing this very stressful and arduous task, the AI answer would have been very different. But that's just the hard-nosed unreconstructed feminist in me. So out of character.

To female majority: Hi! Really? You're not coping? But you're the caring gender?! Have some counselling if you must, but it's a better idea just not to think about it and get on with it. Come on, it's not like a *proper* job.

To male majority: Hi! That really sounds beneath you, man! How about you give the baby to your mom? Problem solved.

Aw, your old mom is asleep?! I'm sure she'll wake up when you put the baby on her lap. Particularly with that stinky diaper! Some snacks and beers will be arriving. Get yourself back on Fortnite. And relax!

Grandmas-A-Gogo

Loads of women can't wait to have grandchildren, because they get the fun of spending time with them, but don't have to do the whole surrogate parenting biz, so they can spoil them. Some women are nervous about being called upon to look after grandchildren because they are anxious that it will be stressful or difficult. But then they find it is a joy they had not expected. My mum was neither of these.

Firstly, she moved a long way from me even before I had contemplated children and then when I had my first daughter at the age of 43, my mum would have been in her late sixties and 150 miles away. She said she would come down and stay for three weeks to help out at the very beginning and duly arrived not long after I was out of hospital. She stayed the first night. And then went home.

In fairness to her, I think she probably wasn't too well at the time and just didn't like staying somewhere a long way from home. Admittedly our house was quite a mess (joke alert!) so perhaps it was the request to clean the fridge. She did say at one point later on that she found children a bit difficult, especially during the non-verbal stage. You may think it's an irony that she worked as a social worker in the area of child protection, and she was probably burnt out, or you may think, 'All the more reason.' Or maybe my mum was at the vanguard of The Rebel Grandma movement. These days women have many plausible reasons for not wanting to take on the care of grandchildren, including valuing freedom and leisure, avoiding physical and emotional burnout, wanting to sidestep arguments about parenting approaches, other responsibilities, and not wanting to be taken advantage of. They may also feel they've done their time. I can understand most of these apart from parenting arguments, because I don't have any grandchildren. Some people change their minds when they meet their grandchildren, as a couple of my friends have, but some don't. It's not a bad thing to acknowledge women have agency to make their own decisions these days, is it really? Rather than not liking children putting you at risk of a spell in prison. It's about bloody time!

One thing many Boomers are being called up to do, as we become sandwiches, is to continue working when we thought we could retire. Now, many of them may be well pissed off the retirement age is climbing faster than ever and people who thought they were going to have a good old lie-down have been stopped in their tracks, pushed back up on their feet like aged old horses and been encouraged to stagger on. However, I'm a bit ambivalent about retirement and whether it's a great idea for everyone. I think staggering it may be a good idea, because sitting in your house listening to *Woman's Hour* discuss issues that applied to you forty years ago isn't the best fun.

In this sandwich scenario it's difficult to make hard and fast rules that suit everyone. If you consider all the different variables at play, trying to cover every base, in an attempt to sort out a problem which is pretty much insurmountable, it is impossible to do something that pleases everyone, although I would be inclined to skew any solution more towards women.

After all, it's not really women who don't do their fair share of managing a household, or who go on to have family after family, sometimes into their nineties (see Rupert Murdoch or Robert De Niro), or leave multiple children round the place without taking any responsibility for them. All right, I'm generalizing and making women sound like saints and men like devils, but old habits die hard and on balance I'm probably nearer the truth than the other way round.

So how will the sandwich generation develop and what can poor knackered, overworked (mainly) women hope for in the future?

I expect things will change again, and as many younger women are opting not to have children, the focus may just shift to older people and how we look after them as family members.

I do think that, because of the changing dynamic and men being generally more involved in the care of children, things will change pretty radically. Women are flourishing in the workplace and even when my daughters were young and at primary school, I did notice a distinct change at pick-up time when far more dads started turning up to collect their children. So, my vision of the future would be that women are the main breadwinners, but instead of coming home and doing the housework, they do *absolutely nothing* and just chill. Because as things stand, the stress is mainly on the older women rather than the men. It may even be, Sandwich Woman, you haven't had time to read this chapter in its entirety. So here is a helpful equation to sum it up:

Number of adult children still at home + their children

+ parents and in-laws requiring different levels of care + hours of sleep lost + funds available for care home + child-care for grandchildren 3 times a week + stress = A Shit Sandwich.

Sorry it's not very sophisticated.

CHAPTER ELEVEN

Have Teabags, Will Travel

So, if your time isn't completely taken up with caring for the younger/older generations, you might be considering getting away from it all . . . I should confess right at the beginning of this chapter that I have never really liked holidays much. Sacrilege, I know. I think this is because, as a child, everything always seemed more tense on holiday. We were probably one of those families who fared better when everyone was doing their own thing. Not easy when you're five years old.

As society grew from villages into towns, transport developed beyond recognition and people were finally granted a right to time off, we gradually began to move for leisure purposes beyond our own immediate towns or cities to spend time by the sea. Back then, it was actually nice to swim in – absolutely no poo at all (apart from the time years ago when a friend of mine's three-year-old had a sneaky one in the sea and I watched as she spent ten minutes trying to retrieve it with a Sainsbury's bag. I can see that on a gameshow of *How To Enjoy Your Holiday*.)

But holidays were not an option for most people in the UK for centuries until a few landmark changes were made to the way that workers were treated. Breaks were considered a luxury and not a necessity, pretty much up to the 1950s and 1960s when people finally got proper holiday pay and someone invented the package holiday, which allowed anyone that was interested to get food poisoning on the cheap in a different country.

We all got a bit bolder in the sixties and seventies when people began to move beyond this country to holiday in that place known as 'the rest of the world'. Although when I was a child, opportunities for foreign holidays for ordinary people didn't really extend much further than the countries next door to them (Wales and Scotland), if they could be afforded at all apart from by the very adventurous and/or filthy rich, and our family could not be described as either of those. I think perhaps the most adventurous holiday we attempted was to a house in France. We went with another family we were friendly with, my mum being particularly friendly with the mother, who was known to have a bit of a sharp tongue. The day after we got there, there was a bit of an argument and my mum's friend made a jokey insulting remark to my dad, which he didn't like, and he slapped her round the face. Then we all went home. After that, my brothers and I found we didn't really go on holiday with other families again.

One thing that I do think was much more sensible in the bygone world was the very limited record people had of their holidays. My grandparents, once they had progressed more towards middle age, would manage one or two grainy black-and-white photos in which they were awkwardly posed on the beach, and it took no longer than a split second to look at them whilst nodding admiringly. Things then got out of hand quite quickly as people progressed to colour photos which, God be praised, did at least have to be developed at a chemist for a merciful week or two. After that, because you could use those bloody awful slides in a projector, we were subjected to being 'entertained' for what seemed like aeons by holiday photos – all those interminable evenings sat in front of a projector, treated to such fascinating pieces of information as 'And here's Uncle Ernie diving into the pool at Butlins', which was always snapped a millisecond too late and featured a pair of somewhat unattractive men's feet disappearing into some murky water.

Now, of course, things have become even more extreme as younger people take shot upon shot of exactly the same thing in a vain attempt to pinpoint the perfect image of themselves, very often in harmony with a dramatic feature of an exotic landscape, like clinging by one fingernail to the top of the Burj Khalifa, risking life and limb for something that will pass through the vision of relatives and friends for no longer than a couple of seconds, may get quite a few likes on their socials and then disappear for ever out of the consciousness of any viewers. So was it really worth the effort?

Yes, I know it's bait for their social media, but doesn't it make more sense for an older person to take these sorts of risks? At least they'll have lived a life if they go plunging off a cliff or disappear off the top of a mountain. My dad once climbed the trickier side of Snowdon in North Wales with some friends in a howling gale, and although they were roped together, they weren't anchored to the ground. When a huge gust blew a couple of the less weighty ones up in the air, someone thankfully managed to drive some sort of curved hammer thing into the earth to secure them. Not a SINGLE BLOODY PICTURE of that. Typical!

Years later, he would take me up the 'easy side of Snowdon', just me and him. I was about eight years old at the time and suggested we should take some water and maybe some food. (I'm not that sensible these days.) He said the café would be open so we wouldn't need to. Well, it wasn't, it was bloody well closed, and there we were, boiling hot, with no water, fuming, and me wishing he'd fall off on the way down. I suppose this might have been when my suspicions were first confirmed that adults weren't always right, particularly male ones! Not to mention if someone says something with enough conviction a lot of people will automatically believe them.

I remember liking holidays when I was a student. They were cheap as anything and, as far as I can remember, nobody felt obliged to travel round Vietnam for six months or learn how to dive in Costa Rica. Greece was our destination of choice: cheap, hot and a delight on Magic Bus, a rickety coach that went all the way to Greece for about six quid, with psychedelics frequently passed between its passengers (though sadly not provided by the bus company). A friend of mine went on Magic Bus to India, got a terrible stomach bug halfway there, the driver refused to keep stopping, so he just had to sit in his sleeping bag for the rest of the journey. Fill in the dots, everyone.

I was never that keen on flying, a fear I inherited from my mum. But eventually I went on a Don't-Be-Scared course my friend and fellow comic Jeff got me for my birthday. He came along too and managed to piss himself laughing the whole way through the experience. The very old woman handing out Valium in the toilet was a complete godsend. (This wasn't part of the course, by the way.) After that I was able to fly to various comedy festivals round the world without disgracing myself by becoming hysterical whenever some turbulence occurred. I never wanted to repeat a horrendous flight back from

Malta when I was actually slapped by a stewardess because I wouldn't calm down. By the way, I was off my face, which was the medical approach I took to my fear of flying in those days. I have tended to see working abroad doing stand-up as a holiday anyway, and it was always easier to tack something onto the end of work rather than go somewhere separately, which meant I could spend a week or so in the Whitsunday Islands, drive to Niagara Falls from Montreal and wander aimlessly round Amsterdam.

Was there a golden age when air travel was not what it is now? I think not. These days we have queues, cancellations, pissed people on flights terrorizing everyone else, people with disabilities being treated very shoddily and stress, stress, stress. With cheapness and accessibility comes frustration and hanging about, but at least more people do have a chance to suck it up and see the world.

Pretty much all that's left to be conquered travel-wise by humanity is other planets, and from what you can see through a telescope there's not much there. So how does this all fit into your outlook as you age? Well, there's no doubt that most people, as they age, allow their horizons to shrink somewhat, limiting their holidays to a bungalow in Pevensey Bay as they head eventually towards the great bungalow in the sky. The end. Oh, OK. I suppose a very small group of older adventurers carry on and make their way across Asia on motorbikes or give ballooning across the Sahara a go. I am not one of those. Never have been and never will be. What is wrong with them? That's very unfair of me – it's probably more appropriate to ask, 'What's wrong with me?'

These days, for a bigger group of ageing people, the options seem almost endless for travel, depending on the size of one's bank balance, sense of adventure, priorities and health.

Let's start with the very basic level of transport: getting buses and coaches. In London, people over 65 get a Freedom Pass which means they can travel gratis anywhere in the city. That's all right if you don't want to go far and be back home for tea, which if you're old and grumpy like me is a good option on most days.

The cliché is that older people love coach trips. I don't know any at all that do. I used to watch groups dismounting from coaches when I was younger and think, 'Poor bastards.' What about if a group of bikers picked you up from your house and did a ton up round the local vicarage lawn. That would certainly have done it for me. I'm probably wildly out of date, though. I'm sure coaches have improved no end since I went on one years ago. A lot of companies that offer coach trips make a point of saying that they are specifically tailored 'for the needs of older people'. I feel like booking a trip just to see what that actually means. Apart from your own personal toilet under the seat, I'm not sure what extras they've added in. A defibrillator? Although they're everywhere these days too. I stayed in Devon a few years ago with a load of mates and we went for a *very* long walk in the woods with the pub as our goal at the end. Of course, the pub was up a very steep hill, and just as you reached the top, some clever clogs had installed a defibrillator, fixed to the wall of the pub. Genius!

I think train travel is probably my favourite mode of transport, especially a sleeper train, although God forbid you are allocated the top bunk for an overnight haul. Obviously, the only worry if you're seeing the UK by train is that you might bump into Michael Portillo.

And now we come to perhaps the most romanticized, moving (not in the emotional sense) entertainment for oldies . . . the cruise! I've only ever been on the Isle of Wight ferry and crossed the Channel a couple of times, but we have occasionally seen the hulking great brutes (cruise ships) called something like *The Massive Empress of The Sewer* that dwarf tower blocks and look like you could push them over.

I have been asked to do a bit of entertainment of the stand-up variety on cruise ships. 'Surely not,' I hear you cry. 'Weren't asked to do a bit of exotic dancing then?' I wouldn't mind doing it for a laugh, but as I think I mentioned, I've inherited my grandma's arthritis, so that would make for an interesting performance. In fact, how about medical or surgical cruises during which you could have treatment for your arthritis, or unwanted bits of you removed in an idyllic setting, maybe with a bit of therapy thrown in if you're not too happy about the fact that you are approaching your demise? Maybe one day there will be euthanasia cruises if you fancied being buried at sea. (I'm sorry, I'm aware I'm sounding flippant here, but the old saying 'You've got to laugh, or you'd cry' seems to sum up so much of the global politics experience currently. And I've always been inclined to laugh at the wrong moments.) Or I could quite happily book on a cruise at any point in the future called 'Get Off Your Face Round the Fjords with a Minor Royal'. I realize I am somewhat singular in my desires, so all of this is unlikely to happen. Perhaps that's for the best.

Let's talk about driving, because with the arrival on the scene of cheaper cars a lot more people can afford to take them anywhere they want. I think the furthest I've driven is Holland and it's not the distance that defeated me, but the added concentration required to negotiate unfamiliar traffic signs and road etiquette on roads abroad and I was only 50 at the time!

Driving a car is a huge issue as you age, because reactions are slowing, sight is deteriorating, priorities on roads are changing and unless you are a batty Agatha Christie detective aged 85 in a Morris Minor, your ability to negotiate country roads or city junctions will become enormously compromised as your age advances.

Don't even get me started on the fact that there are

now cars with headlights so bright they probably double up as interrogation tools and (surprise, surprise) they are particularly difficult for the over-fifties to negotiate. This is another thing to add to the list of older people's potential driving difficulties, and as this list grows, it is for these reasons that there is a movement to either remove older people's licences altogether at a certain age or, at least, to enforce driving tests more frequently after a certain age. I know that cars that drive themselves are already on the road in the very late stage of being perfected, but I like driving and I want to do it myself. I'm also prepared to accept at some point that my driving skills may not be adequate, and then I will get out of the car, but not without a fist fight.

We have yet to alight on the caravan, the moving house traditionally beloved of older people. So beloved, in fact, that some people live in static ones without any wheels when they go on holiday. Add to these camper vans, which are more acceptable to younger people, who obviously feel that caravans are tainted with a whiff of the codger.

It has always looked to me like you needed a degree in mechanical engineering to hook a caravan and car together. We had a caravan for a bit when I was a child and my parents were still quite young. It didn't last very long and what really used to piss me off was that you couldn't sit in them and do whatever you liked while your dad was driving along. Well, I was only about seven years old and not really an afficionado of road safety, not to mention how caravans do tend to be the vehicles-non-grata of the roads.

I very rarely sit around and wonder what caravans of the future will be like. (I'm sure that's not a surprise to anyone.) But hopefully a robot will attach them to your car for you, although I suspect they might disappear altogether in favour of massive US-type motor homes. Maybe in the future we might have flying motor homes, which can take you wherever you want, and if your health is not too good, you could have a support nurse attached in a pod on the side for emergencies or just call them up as a hologram if you take a turn for the worse.

I would imagine, considering the way tech is advancing at a terrifying rate, you can probably now sit at home with a VR headset on and climb Everest without even having to move. I wish I'd had the technology as an eight-year-old to do an online search and find out the opening times of that bloody café.

MY BUCKET LIST

The name 'bucket list' is derived from the charming phrase 'kicking the bucket'. And 'kicking the bucket' has several possible origins to pick from, ranging from animal slaughter to suicide. Sorry, there don't seem to be any charming derivations that mention bunnies or teddies.

People's bucket lists are individual choices for taking in dramatic sights and scenery, experiences, learning a language or eating food somewhere else other than your local chippie. A lot of people used to travel north to the frozen wastes of Iceland and the like, but recently those friendly Northern Lights have trundled down as far as Norfolk, which is handy in terms of travel and accommodation as I could theoretically go there and back in a day. Maybe you think I'm being somewhat unromantic, but honestly, how long can you genuinely stand there and look at a whirling tableau of (admittedly lovely) colours and shapes in the sky before you start getting a map up on your phone and looking for the nearest pub.

So, I'm going to start with a couple of things that could easily be on someone's bucket list, which I can tell you *aren't* worth the effort.

Firstly, I have eaten a piece of the 'best chocolate in the world'. In other words, it was voted for by some ultra-refined taste buds belonging to chocolate experts for the numerous awards panels round the world. For a start, it wasn't milk chocolate, so that's ruled out 98 per cent of you, including me, philistine that I am. So, unless you're interested and it's free, I'd get some common or garden Dairy Milk type stuff instead.

Secondly, I have been to Vienna, which is very popular as a stand-out cultural experience for bucket-listers. We went to the opera where I was nearly thrown out because I had some very unladylike boots on with steel toecaps. Like I was going to kick off at the opera? Anyway, they let me in eventually. The plot was totally unintelligible, and I couldn't understand a bloody word of it. That's the problem with letting philistines into an opera house.

The other bucket-listy thing that everyone wants to experience in Vienna is the huge Wiener Riesenrad - a giant Ferris wheel with little cabins like workmen's huts hanging off its structure. It lays out an incredible view of Vienna below and I was looking forward to creating the equivalent of an Instagram post, i.e. three blurry photos. It was closed for repairs, bloody typical. But the incident that nearly pulled it all back for me was an encounter in the hotel after dinner when I was approached by a woman in her eighties, dressed in a long brown satin gown with masses of cleavage on show, dripping in diamonds, with a tiara on her head. She was quite pissed, knew who I was and was effusively complimentary. I glanced at her very expensive dress. It had chicken soup all down it. I think it was at that point that I knew what sort of old lady I wanted to be.

So, I have decided to have a crack at an alternative bucket list that doesn't involve circumnavigating the globe or going somewhere very high (the destination, not me).

My alternative bucket list

- Learning to type on my phone with my thumbs. Not easy because they are the wrong way round, known colloquially as 'murderer's thumbs'. In days gone by, these thumbs were branded as a mark of a primitive disposition and a sign of impulsive and unsophisticated thinking. Spot on! Typing with my thumbs instead of jabbing with one digit will be a victory for the one-fingered generation and will hold off the derision of my daughters.

- Extending my repertoire for karaoke from one to two songs. Currently, it's 'Three Lions' and I growl it. Quite fancy adding 'Nessun Dorma'.

- Wearing a proper lady's dress out to an event without looking like a cross between the Archbishop of Canterbury and a duvet. That's never going to happen.

- Wing walking. Hahaha, not really.

CHAPTER TWELVE
Bedpans and Dipsticks

Hospitals and those who work in them are really about the best of humanity. OK, some hospitals aren't perfect, particularly clean, or staffed 100 per cent with perfect angels, but I still think they are to be admired enormously. And not just by standing on your doorstep *clapping*.

The first hospital in the UK was St Bartholomew's which was opened in 1123 for the benefit of the sick, the poor and pilgrims. Not many of the latter around these days at Bart's, I would imagine, as not many people I can think of would want to make a pilgrimage from anywhere to central London, although sometimes it feels like it, just using public transport. And I can't imagine that nuns were particularly qualified to minister to the sick at that time, apart from making a cup of tea, giving people a wash and saying a prayer for the patients. That's still better than a kick up the arse though.

As you age, you are more likely to progress from being

a mere acquaintance of hospitals to, if not a regular visitor, then more of an occasional one. You only need to worry if you get an award for regular attendance.

Many older people find themselves in hospital, and more likely these days in a hospital corridor, but if I was very ill, I'd still rather be in a hospital corridor than at home. I mean, the dog's not going to do anything if I have another cardiac arrest, is she? Although, having said that, I am maybe being a bit unfair on dogs. On Instagram, there are simply *loads* of posts that show dogs, particularly, saving babies from appalling injury by pulling them or pushing them away from danger. The problem with this is I have absolutely no idea which ones, if any, are real and which ones are AI. Even I know, however, that the dogs wearing hats, telling each other jokes and then having a good laugh together are very unlikely to be real dogs. Sadly.

Over the years, hospitals have morphed into many different types of institutions. I have a particular interest in the Bethlem Royal Hospital, which treats those with mental health issues and was originally housed in The Priory of St Mary of Bethlehem, on the site of what is now Liverpool Street Station, and was later moved to The Imperial War Museum in Lambeth. With those high ceilings it must have been a bugger to heat, and no global warming to help them out then.

I worked at the Bethlem Royal in the 1970s on the site where it eventually settled for good and spent some of my time there on a ward for the elderly. I seem to recall the nurse in charge was quite a bit more terrifying than the patients. The main thing I can remember about my time there was that some research was being carried out on some of the patients and it involved a medication being administered which caused the patients to give off a very strong odour, sort of fishy and eggy at the same time. Those poor people. It seemed to me immaterial in some ways whether it made them any better or not, because nobody felt inclined to go near them. And so, the search goes on for a 'cure' for dementia. But we're edging towards it quite slowly and it seems that all we can hope for at the moment is being able to delay some of the symptoms.

Things changed for most in this country with the establishment of the dear old NHS on 5 July 1948 and it's now in its late seventies, so is creaking in a similar way to an equivalent human of that age.

I've had the pleasure of being a hospital patient on a few occasions and perhaps the weirdest experience was totally down to my stupidity. I was dyeing my hair and couldn't be arsed to do a patch test (I think you see where this is going). This is where you dab a bit of dye on your wrist and wait and see whether a poisonous cauliflower or something similar grows on it overnight. I was alerted to the issue by being woken in the middle of the night because it felt like my head was on fire. My scalp was burning and seemed to be squirting something or other from every pore. My rather pointless solution was to stick myself in a cold shower, rinse my flaming head and go back to bed. I woke up a few hours later and realized I could barely see.

What I did manage to spot when I looked in the mirror was that my face had swollen up to twice its normal size, my eyelids were so puffy they were about to close and I didn't recognize myself. I managed to call a friend, and he suggested that we head to the local A&E, which we did. Another friend joined us, so I had two men with me, both comedians, so they obviously thought, 'We'll get a good ten minutes of new material out of this,' which is what every comedian does whenever anything mildly unusual happens.

I sat in A&E while they went off to get coffee. The nursing staff obviously thought the swelling had affected my ears, because they discussed me quite loudly, seemingly unaware I could hear every word. Having not even been assessed at that point, I realized that they had assumed one of the two people I was with was my partner and he had beaten me up. They even discussed the fact that both of my escorts could have done it together. I quite enjoyed it; it was like listening to a soap. Reasonably speedily I was taken off into a cubicle, and it soon became apparent to the 11-year-old doctor that it was an allergic reaction, so I was immediately given a steroid injection and taken off to a ward to be admitted.

I couldn't see for the first day or so, so every sound was

magnified, including people sniggering at the end of my bed. And all day I could hear a woman's voice shouting, 'Please kill me,' over and over again. Various muted (and not so muted) shouts of 'Shut up!' floated through the air, or entreaties like, 'Nurse, make her be quiet!' The nurse had obviously tried and not succeeded, because the pleas continued. When I eventually managed to see properly, I saw a very elderly lady who was deaf and blind, had no real idea of where she was and was absolutely tormented. I just felt so sorry for her. I think of that poor woman now and again and how utterly powerless she must have felt and wonder what happened to her.

As well as being a real nurse back in the day I also did three series as a pretend nurse in a show called *Getting On*. This presented us with the challenge of writing *yet another* series set in a hospital, coupled with getting the tone of resigned weariness and pessimism right, not to mention making it funny. Many of the situations in it were ones that I had experienced myself or heard of through friends. Each series was filmed at a different hospital, the most difficult being an empty hospital in the East End in the middle of a very cold winter with snow on the ground. So, while the crew had puffa jackets, scarves and hats on, we were in short-sleeved nurses' dresses. At least the supporting artistes, all older women, were in bed with blankets.

Many people would come up to us with comments or suggestions, and I particularly remember quite an elderly woman coming up to me in the street after series 2 and asking if we would consider including a storyline about a real man who had been in a bed next to her in hospital and who wouldn't stop masturbating. We did actually give that one a miss.

All my experiences in real and imaginary hospitals have sent me the very firm message that absolutely anything can happen and it's all in a day's work. Being a pretend nurse, however, is so much easier than being a real one.

One group of older people who become trapped in hospital and are known informally and somewhat disrespectfully as 'bed blockers' are the unwitting victims of the system. I don't think that 'bed blockers' was ever in any way an official or acceptable phrase used by the NHS, and I hope that label never reaches the ears of the people in question, because there is a lot of shame attached to it, as if it is the fault of the individuals themselves. And I don't mean, 'Oh, what a shame they're a bed blocker.' These patients are, of course, awarded that charming designation because they are occupying a bed when they don't really need one. 'Bed blockers' are inevitably older people who cannot be cared for at home, either because there is no one at home to meet their needs, or those needs are too complex for relatives or carers visiting up to a few times a day. Many years ago, before residential homes became a thing, people just had to accommodate an elderly relative as best they could and, of course, given what medical care was available in those days, one would imagine the poor old relative wouldn't last that long anyway. This begs a question to contemplate elsewhere about whether we're living too long, and if so, what to do about it.

So, these poor so-called 'bed blockers' lie pointlessly in hospital until a local authority can take them into one of their residential facilities and pay for them, or relatives can stump up thousands of pounds a week to cover the cost of a private home or private care in their own home. Being in hospital is grim at the best of times, but an extended stay when no one really wants you there must be grimmer, particularly since Covid.

To me this seems to be a theme running through the care of older people, that they are in many ways obstacles that need to be cleared out of the way to allow someone with more pressing problems to take their place.

I suppose, though, I am talking about a time thirty or so years ago and hospitals, although they faced difficult challenges, did not have the endless queues of ambulances outside A&E, or corridors lined with beds containing people who need a bed but can't get one on a ward just yet. Was it idyllic in the NHS pre-Covid? Probably not, but when one thinks of the sheer volume of money wasted during Covid, the poor decisions, the backhanders to mates, and the huge temporary hospitals left empty, because they could not be staffed by the right specialist nurses, one would think that now the Covid epidemic is over things would gradually go back to normal, but they haven't. (Can I shut up about politics now, I hear you cry? I will, honestly. In a minute.) I think there are many reasons for this, ranging from nurses leaving the profession (and who could blame them?) to older people with mixed complex conditions becoming more common, to name just a couple.

You may think that it's time that we moved to a system like they have in the US where all healthcare is managed by private insurance. Roughly 8 per cent of people in the US do not have private health insurance, which doesn't sound too bad until you realize that is approximately 26–27 million people. And they either rely on A&E, apply for something called Medicaid or use community health centres. Not dissimilar to dentistry over here.

I think that one of the most damaging factors for the NHS is that it does not lie outside the political, so every time a different government is voted in, sweeping changes are made and money is added or subtracted depending on who is in power, not to mention the money spent reorganizing the whole bloody system first! Nothing ever gets a proper chance to develop before the next lot sweep in and make significant changes *again*. And then Covid comes along, or a war, or the world order changes, or a new health secretary comes in and says all the wards have got to be painted green, and other areas need to be prioritized. Why not take the NHS out of the mix for a bit and agree to leave it alone for twenty years, just to give it a chance to settle down, rather than shuffling it every five years? I'm sure this has been considered on occasion, but it's very unlikely the opposing parties would ever agree a compromise that suited everyone. Hey, who would have thought that might ever work?

So, what can we expect healthcare to be like in the future? Well, unsurprisingly, the predictions go down the AI route. AI will analyse data and speed up disease detection, so they say. Well, that could mean anything from personal handheld whole-body scanners which send the data straight off to a boffin hunched over a computer (sorry, I love that 'boffin' word), to your GP updating their laptop from 2015.

Also, I think there's no doubt that at some point robots will take over minor surgery from humans and visit you at home: 'I've got the district robot coming to do my ingrowing toenails, Doris. Better put the kettle on.'

And apparently medicine will be more personalized. That could be antibiotics in your favourite colours or your own individually designed care plan distributed to every possible medic who might come into your orbit ever.

There will be a shift to prevention and home care. This mantra is trotted out regularly, and it's all very well if you have a nice house, but what about the people whose homes are messy, unheated, lonely or sliding down a cliff?

A lot of people quite like going to hospital so they don't have to do the hoovering for a bit and get regularly fed.

My penultimate prediction for the future of healthcare is that video consultations will continue to grow. Great. Personally, I have always hated any kind of video consultation. For a start, you've got to make a bit of an effort, unless you do jumper on top and pyjama trousers and slippers on the bottom. What if you've got to display the affected bit of yourself? Imagine trying to get your haemorrhoids into the picture . . .

And finally, 'smart wearables' will track your health in real time. God only knows whether anyone over the age of 65 will even know what that means, let alone be able to figure out how to manage them and direct the information to the correct health professional. 'Grandma, you've just sent me all your blood pressure readings for the last week!' Grandma: 'Well, thank God I didn't send them to Grandad.'

In the meantime, I'm very interested in the idea of influencers and the like seeming to be perfectly comfortable with continuing to post stuff even when they are in hospital. Often one is treated to the pale-looking celeb doing their best to summon up a smile but still looking perfectly presentable, regaling us with tales of their latest surgery or presenting their new baby to the world. Quite a lot of people look an absolute wreck when they're in hospital and tempted as I am to make a feature of that when I'm in there again, I just can't imagine making any effort whatsoever. As I age, I intend to make even less effort, if that's possible, so unless I want to influence people by doing an impression of a 'before' photo on the long road to recovery, which I can't imagine anyone would want to see, I'll stay away from social media. In fairness, as yet, I have been unable to find an influencer sitting on a commode, but I'm sure that's just because I'm not trying hard enough.

CHAPTER THIRTEEN
Ageing in Public

Can you moan about being treated badly by the press when you have a successful career?

Once upon a time, children, a nasty lady 'celebrity' would have a lovely life swanning around, earning loads of money and not giving a toss about anyone except themselves. It was very important that the lady celebrities kept themselves looking very nice for the public and didn't say rude or controversial things. And, if they didn't behave themselves or do what they were told and didn't make the effort to look nice *all* the time, the newspapers were very, very cross indeed and were forced to show the public just how much these ladies had let themselves go. On the other hand, male celebrities in the public eye weren't quite so scrutinized. As we all know, 'boys will be boys', so unless they were papped lying face down in a pile of Class A nobody minded too much if they got a bit more out of control and enjoyed themselves.

This is how it seemed to me when I first started doing stand-up. The contract between the press and so-called celebrities was all about a mutually rewarding relationship. Ish.

However, as social media has gradually invaded almost everyone's lives, the balance has shifted. Social media is doing the work of the press for them to some extent, and I think celebrities are being made to feel they must open themselves up to their fans or, to use a charming ancient phrase, 'spill their guts' ad nauseam, as it were. This has now evolved into a race of relevance which is accelerating at a terrifying pace, and I feel sorry for people who are sliding down the sides of what is a volcano. They would probably think what they're doing is preferable to my constant social media avoidance, or as my daughter might say, 'Mum, you haven't posted anything for three weeks, it makes you look like you don't care.' I don't!

It sometimes seems as if we cannot get enough of famous people and we all want to be in a tribe. Their lives were traditionally no-go areas to the public, and I think that the openness some people in the public eye have displayed is to the detriment of the many people who would quite like to have a reasonable balance between their private and public lives and keep to themselves at times.

Briefly, press intrusion was pretty rare in the early part

of the twentieth century. Then a group known (not in the slightest bit) fondly as the paparazzi were born in Italy and large-scale stalking of celebrities and newsworthy individuals began in earnest.

I found the whole 'public eye' thing quite difficult to get used to as there seems to be some sort of hidden agenda which dictates the approach of the press in terms of fitting you into a narrative, for example, 'spoilt brat' or 'full of themselves'. If you have any idea what this hidden agenda is, then you can learn how to manage yourself in the public eye. The only contact I had with the press when I was a nurse was when a journalist came to observe our work in the emergency clinic where I worked in south London. She did at one point ask to come into a room when someone who'd been brought in by the police was being assessed by a psychiatrist. Because of the man's privacy, this request was denied. However, she ignored this and tried to barge in anyway while we were all in there. I attempted to shut the door before she got into the room but unfortunately ended up shutting the door on her head. At least it stopped her in her tracks. I also had some brief fame as a child. I was probably about nine years old and witnessed a teenage boy setting fire to a haystack, watching it start to burn and then running away. I ran to the nearest phone box and dialled 999 and the fire brigade arrived to put out the fire. I was a local hero and a photo of me sitting on my dad's lap in my dressing gown appeared in the local paper. I quite enjoyed the fuss for a couple of days.

However, after this promising start, I seemed to be held up later down the line by the press as some sort of universal example of self-neglect, so not much will change as I get older! I once appeared in an article on the opposite page to an actor called Felicity Kendall, who, it was noted, underneath a charming picture of the woman herself, always looked very feminine and well-dressed, whereas I was designated as 'doesn't care'. And I didn't really.

The eventual solution was to stop reading any newspapers. That solution worked well for a bit, but for some reason, and I've spoken to other performers about this, 'friends' and acquaintances always seem to think reporting back the latest insult in the press to you is somehow helpful. Well, it isn't particularly, and even worse when someone half tells you, 'I'm so sorry about what they called you in the paper.' Unfortunately, when I had that incomplete information, I felt compelled to find out and I'm sure you can guess it was never going to be 'looked too thin' or 'a rare natural beauty'. No, phrases like 'hideous old boiler' abounded or 'bloated' this and 'ugly' that. I could kind of cope with this, but not when my mum was told similar by 'friends'. Insult bingo is not a good game to get involved in and eventually I just had to tell people not to mention anything to me, not least because a tiny number did seem to be getting a smidgeon of satisfaction out of keeping me in my place.

Relationships, weddings and babies are all things the press get quite excited about, and they are very good at catching you, a relative innocent at the beginning of your career, and manipulating you into providing something that will sell papers. We managed pretty well to keep our wedding quiet, but two friends nearly blew it. One, when asked in the flower shop who was getting married, panicked and said, 'I am,' and then couldn't remember the name of the church. Another got in the car from a hotel and when asked where she wanted to go, similarly panicked and refused to tell the driver. She did eventually.

Near the beginning of what I'm going to call my comedy 'journey', while it seemed to me the press were making up their minds about how to portray me as an individual, I was coming out of a restaurant called The Ivy where quite a few paparazzi skulked about outside, hoping for a picture with earning potential. I came out alone and a photographer who I came to recognize stopped me, said he hadn't sold a picture for ages and would I mind holding my bag in front of my face. Well, obviously, I thought it was a bit weird, but with my people-pleasing hat on, I went along with it. The next day in one of the tabloids there was a picture of me with aforementioned bag covering my face and a picture of Princess

Diana holding a bag in front of her face with the tagline above it, *Which one of these is a princess?* Yep, I was well and truly skewered by that one and launched on the path to becoming a hard-bitten cynic, which actually, folks, I already was.

I realize I was/am at a very low level of scrutiny compared to many others in the business, whose lives seemed to consist of them travelling between cars and buildings with blankets, coats, and, yes, even bags over their heads. For them the scrutiny is relentless and never stops. For me, it stopped some levels below that and ebbed and flowed depending on whether I'd said anything controversial, which included doing jokes that were considered unacceptable, or upsetting someone further up the pecking order.

The main area in which women were, and continue to be, particularly fair game is their looks, and although men are enduring increasing scrutiny, it is still nowhere near the level that women have put up with. Let's be honest, it doesn't matter one tiny little jot whether as a female comic you are lovely to look at or not. People either laugh or they don't, thank God. However, I do think that how you look does determine the course of your career in both acting and comedy. Actors, depending on their age and how they look, will tend either to be given leading roles or take character parts. Some comics stick to stand-up, others move sideways into acting.

Comedy encompasses the whole range of human shapes and sizes and ultimately it comes down to how much people laugh.

I am and always have been a pragmatist – I can't be arsed to put the time into being thinner and lovelier. I'm not saying it's the only variable but for a long time for women it was quite an important one. I have noticed that showbiz lately seems to require men to be more attractive than they used to be too. The lookers are going further. So, at least things are becoming more even. Happy to see the back of the days where a show I did in Edinburgh with two male comics was reviewed as having one 'cheeky Cockney', one dour Irishman, and I was simply 'fat'. Factually correct, I suppose, if not the best review I've ever had.

Fatness is big news! Literally! Women carrying some weight are always considered to be lacking in willpower, greedy, unpleasant to look at and eminently easily dismissed. Despite a movement amongst the younger members of society, inevitably negative attitudes cling on.

More recently it seems like the entire nation is dropping pounds at an alarming rate. This is because of the introduction into the shrinkage industry of weight loss injections, which work extremely well and knock loads of bulk off very quickly. These injections apparently 'calm the food noise'. And food shouts so loudly to some people. 'Hello, I'm a doughnut! Eat me!' I notice that lettuce keeps very quiet in my world. The people who manufacture the various types of weight loss jabs have certainly done very well out of them and when they started selling very well, hey presto! up went the price.

'Where's the catch with weight loss jabs?' I hear you ask. Hmm. Well, they're apparently frowned upon because that's too easy if you're in the public eye and you need to demonstrate you have struggled through some pain. The gastric band phenomenon was the same. I remember a couple of high-profile celeb people having to deny they had lost weight through the gastric band route. Endless speculation abounded on social media and those boring things made of paper that some people still use . . . oh yes, magazines. Really, who gives a toss? It's bad enough to have to answer any question about change in appearance, and the wrong conclusion is constantly jumped to, as several serious illnesses may also cause you to lose weight. And I think people are much leakier about info these days. I plan to be leakier for different reasons, not least because of 'bulky pee pants'.

In the 1970s and 1980s, some of the people looking not to have an appetite had to be content with amphetamine-based drugs like Tenuate Dospan. This was effective, highly addictive and possibly a tiny bit enjoyable, so it disappeared from the treatment menu very quickly. There were also things called 'Ayds' (I kid you not) and they eventually fell out of favour in the 1980s, hardly surprisingly, because of the AIDS epidemic. Then there were various liquid things like milkshakes which didn't even taste that nice. Yes, I think I might have tasted them all at one time or another.

There is some evidence that weight loss injections don't work long term, but don't worry, someone will invent something else before you can say 'cronut', and if you're using whatever this treatment is, there will be plenty of photographic evidence to track your shrinking, wrinkling figure with some glee.

So, does the population want people in the public eye to suffer? Yes, I imagine some do, if X and TikTok are anything to go by. It's part of the role not to complain about *anything*. And believe you me, I do try! I'm saving most of my moaning for when I'm a bit older, as that's our job.

Other areas that are unacceptable for male and female celebrities as they age are teeth that do not dazzle like spotlights. Many remortgage their house and see a dentist in this country, others head for Turkey. It's still not cheap and gives the phrase, 'Turkey for Christmas' a whole new meaning.

Bosoms are an issue for a lot of women. They're too big, too small, different sizes, non-existent, pointing in the wrong direction or too droopy. Yes, it's a nightmare.

Does anyone ever make those sorts of comments about testicles? No, because men are not encouraged to have them on show. I did know one comic whose party trick was to put a pair of glasses on his testicles. That was his impression of General de Gaulle, and it was uncanny.

Hair does not behave itself as you age. Pubic hair buggers off on holiday, some of it stopping for an extended break on your face. Head hair thins out, falls off or becomes the colour of nicotine-stained fingers. Sadly, the comb-over is no longer with us, so it's not an option for men to do an impression of some seventies blokes any more. Just as well. Wigs are slightly more realistic and no longer look like a nest has dropped out of a tree onto your head, and of course hair transplants are becoming ever more popular. I do feel that in the ageing stakes, men have a lot to contend with too. Bald, bosomy and beer-gutty isn't much of a future to look forward to, is it? I'll let you know how it goes.

Clickbait

Let's have a brief look at the way in which many older celebrities (and they are mainly older women, but not exclusively) are used to entertain scrollers and good old-fashioned 'readers' as they head away from their youth. The two main groups under the most intense scrutiny are the very naughty older celebrities who have dared to age 'badly', i.e. all on their own with no intervention, or the group whose cosmetic surgery has gone wrong. When you view these ageing celebrities, the rules dictate that you must stare in wonder at some poor old 'hag' who has ignored her multiplying wrinkles with the temerity to not be bothered about it. (Guilty.)

These images are inevitably presented under the general heading of 'What do they look like now?' You will first see a picture of them when they were a young attractive person before being urged to trawl through many pictures to see 'what they look like now' and you will arrive at shrivelled, face-melty portraits of someone who has 'not aged well'. It's most reminiscent of circus performers like the bearded lady. Gawp, gawp, gawp! In fact, maybe I could run away to the circus when my beard gets a bit more established.

It's a cruel spectator sport trying to hunt down ageing people online and do the equivalent of pointing and laughing. I did this once and then felt immediately tainted by it and, incidentally, I didn't laugh. There are people whose facial surgery went wrong, who have put on loads of weight, men who have lost hair and yet everyone behaves as if certain political figures look close to a human, because power overrides all, takes years off you.

Perhaps older people need relatives and friends to be

more brutally honest about things that are obvious, but too embarrassing to mention. Mine already do as I extricate a baked bean from my hair from time to time. I do warm to unashamedly proper old, old people (if you see what I mean). Besides, the effort of keeping yourself looking pristine, without a smear of brown sauce on your cardy or chocolate round your mouth, is exhausting. I think a small wing mirror curving out from your shoulder would be very handy – regular glances would reveal any transgressions down your front, and you could spot people you don't want to talk to approaching from the rear and pretend to have a heart attack. Either that or someone with a dustpan and brush following you around armed with a handy wet wipe or two.

Thankfully I'm not really one of those people who feels the strong pull of a premiere or an awards ceremony. 'Well, that's good 'cause you hardly ever get any awards,' I hear you cry. Good point. If I did go to them, I would definitely commit some of the faux pas I have witnessed in the past, often blandly described as a 'wardrobe malfunction'. These are where the camera-bearing paparazzi gather in the vain hope that someone who rarely ventures out might be coming along to get a life-time achievement award and have their flies undone or their wig on the incline.

Well-respected stars, even if they have retired into anonymity, cannot escape press obsession if something happens that looks wrong. People whose facelifts have gone wrong, who are addicted to drugs, people who overdo the weight loss jabs which maybe they didn't even need in the first place; there are so many potential dangers to trip you up. Even when they've moved on to the next world, it is inescapable. Makes me want to quote my grandma: 'What is the world coming to?' Answers on a very big postcard, please.

CHAPTER FOURTEEN

'An Active Retirement'

For some reason this phrase makes me shudder. I have visions of posh women in their eighties in tweedy slacks striding out across some moors somewhere, 'fit as fiddles' (hate that phrase too), probably trying to shoot things. Everyone knows the right things to do to give yourself the best chance to live a long time, and most people dread following the advice to the letter more than dying young anyway. Well, not everyone: me. This is because the phrase 'everything in moderation' fills me with equal horror. I have tried to be an 'in moderation' person for most of my life. All right, I haven't 'tried' as such, but I have thought about it very hard.

In Victorian times, long before anyone thought older people might want to organize their leisure time for themselves in their 'twilight years', there weren't any opportunities for elderly fun because older people's lives were dominated by work instead (apart from the wealthy, of course). And to employ a big dollop of understatement, that wasn't great, because work was very hard, days were long and they couldn't afford to do anything interesting when they had free time because they hardly had any, they were way too knackered, or they were at death's door. I'm talking mainly about poorer people here.

Most people as they aged worked until they dropped. They were then presumably propped up somewhere at home. That sounds like a better prospect than being banished to many residential homes. Not because they're awful, but they're different, and choice and independence disappears. For many of the poorest people, however, a decline into poverty was common if they stopped working. If they could not rely on their family or charity, they were often forced into workhouses. Men and women were segregated and much of the work involved unravelling old tarred ropes. If you could manage something a bit more physical, you could have a go at breaking stones. Can't say I've ever thought to myself, 'Hm, I really fancy unravelling an old tarred rope – no, perhaps not, maybe I'll have a go at breaking some stones instead.' Leisure time was not a complete no-no, with pubs and music halls flourishing if you had a bit of spare cash, but life wasn't intended ever to be much fun for the lower working classes in Victorian times. That's why lots of religious types had to go around telling people they'd get their reward in heaven.

This grim existence for older people changed a bit

for the better in the early twentieth century when 70 was brought in as the first pension age, which begs the question: were most older people living past the age of 70 then? I think not. Pension age eventually dropped to 60 for women and 65 for men, but has recently been climbing again as governments struggle to afford the rising numbers of old people who won't conform to the statistics and shuffle off this mortal coil at a reasonable age to suit available funds. Or, as Scrooge in *A Christmas Carol* said, 'Maybe they had better die and reduce the surplus population.' But that was before he turned into a decent, lovely person.

Activities

We have now morphed into a society which offers endless activities for retirees, from bingo to world cruises, although a vast number of people shun all of them for economic and social reasons. A cursory search of the internet with the question, 'What do old people like doing?' has thrown up some things that I can't ever imagine myself doing or ever wanting to do. We'll start with the more common retirement activities and I'm going to rate them based on the probability, percentage wise, of me indulging in such activities should I ever be forced to retire.

Gardening

Rating: 20 per cent. This 20 per cent entirely covers sitting in the garden when someone has finished the gardening.

Gardening seems to come up a lot and it's the law if you are beyond retirement age that you must 'potter' in your garden if you have one. Not sure how 'pottering' differs from actual gardening though. I sense it means that you don't get involved in the heavier side of gardening, so no digging, back-breaking weeding or giving people the chance to buy you flowery kneepads or similar when they've run out of birthday present ideas. I'd like the garden to look nice, but can't be bothered to put the work in. It's probably like pottering in the kitchen where you don't really do much, and certainly don't go down the road of baking, cooking or anything very domesticated, apart from the bare minimum, which I very much favour.

Another seemingly popular activity for older people is to go and have 'a stroll' round a great big garden attached to a stately home. 'Strolling' is mainly an older person word too, isn't it? Wandering about with no real intended aim is a cherished pastime for some older people, but not me, guv'nor.

The good bit about having a lovely garden is sitting in it and vegetating, not growing the bloody things. As well as this, so much of gardening is very, very boring.

It's laborious, doesn't always produce what you want, and most of it is so repetitive. I say this in the full knowledge that my best friend absolutely *loves* gardening, and her garden does look lovely, but I'd rather watch an episode of *The Traitors* or do a cryptic crossword.

I think having been brought up in the country has forever imprinted a certain tangled wildness of growth into my head and I love rambling plants and lots of trees. (Just as well.) Also, I can't understand why you would want to grow vegetables, bearing in mind that creatures can lick them, disease can affect them, rain can drown them and you could go to a shop and buy some, without having had to deal with any of the former.

Allotment gardening

Rating: 0.7 per cent. Far too back-breaking and allotment chit-chat is way beyond my skill set.

For a while, when my dad lived near me, he had an allotment in a lovely spot in south London. (He hadn't been put off by the donkeys eating all his beloved tiny Christmas trees when I was a kid.) The view over London was glorious, but I can't really think of anything else about it that attracted me. There were lots of perfectly friendly old blokes who were very chatty (the kind who scratch their foreheads and the rim of their cap moves up a few inches). These guys like nothing better than to discuss in meticulous, torturous detail the progress of their runner beans and courgettes. (Courgettes are for what exactly? It is certainly not eating, in my opinion.)

When my dad moved away, he suggested I take over his allotment. He seemed so keen, that I was unable to say no. Even though I seem like a man-hating harridan to many, I am an unreconstructed people-pleaser part-time, so I caved in very easily even though hours spent at an allotment with lots of old geezers wasn't really part of my life plan.

I then had to come up with a scheme to manage my allotment patch by making it as easy as possible with the minimum amount of effort, and then planned to tell my dad some time later that I was too busy to keep it up. So, what to grow? That was easy, something nice to eat that didn't require too much thinking about. And something to brighten the allotment up a bit. Well, I love potatoes, whether that's down to my Irish heritage or not, and they sounded easy enough to grow, so I allotted my allotment half for potatoes and, to brighten it up, flowers. With potatoes, you just need to sling them in the ground, no home-made tied-together sticks for runner beans to ramble over, or a complicated netting arrangement to protect raspberries. And the flowers? Somewhat hit and miss in the sense of putting some seeds in the ground and seeing what happens, because I've never had the patience to read a gardening book. Invariably, three lines in, there will be a word I don't understand or an instruction that just seems too much of a faff and I'll give up.

Well, of course it all went wrong. The flowers didn't really like the soil, the potatoes had little holes bored into them by some weevil-type things and the weather was never brilliant when I went up there, not to mention the old blokes turning ever so slightly hostile when they saw the state my allotment was in, ruining the general effect of their hard work, and that ended any ambitions I might have had to be a gardener or allotmenteer.

Flower Arranging

Rating: 0.5 per cent. No artistic skill whatsoever, added to no patience.

I think perhaps my allotment experience might also have had some influence on my reluctance to become a champion flower arranger, but this is also linked to the fact that even if I had arranged a vase of flowers perfectly I probably wouldn't realize it, as my approach tends to be: shove them in and if they look a bit lop-sided then wiggle them around a bit. Eat your heart out, Chelsea Flower Show judges. I think some people just have an eye for what looks good. My artistic skills are zero. I don't think I have that eye in any sense of the word. I am one of those annoying people who resolutely declares, 'I know what I like,' but if I had to say why, I don't think I could come up with anything. And that's the reason I don't tend to do flower arranging in my spare time.

Sewing

Rating: 0.6 per cent. The only thing I've ever learned about sewing is what thimbles are for.

Let's do proper lady home crafts now. I had my first encounter with the art of sewing, if you can call it that, at the age of about 12 at secondary school when we had to make a blouse. A blouse? I'd never even worn one! Anyway, there was no other exciting choice, like competitive duck herding. No, it was Latin and sewing for me. Weirdly, I really liked Latin. We did Caesar's Gallic wars, and I loved all that 'mounting the ramparts' and 'sending despatches to Cicero'. It made me realize that in many ways, it's all about the teacher rather than the subject. The teacher we had for Latin was gentle, sweet-natured and seemed really old to us when she was probably about 35. She looked so old to us, in fact, I often wondered if she spoke Latin at home. And it was ironic when she was gently talking battles all the time, whereas the teacher for needlework was as fierce as anything.

My mum went out and bought me some material which was flowery and feminine and there was nothing I could do about it, so I soldiered on in a completely cack-handed way and produced something that, to me, looked like a tablecloth with two arms and the odd button on it. I found sewing machines lethal and I am proud to say I never wore that blouse, unless I was trying to spill things down it, and was eventually rewarded when at some point dusters were born out of it. Ironic really, because I think I would have been better at making dusters. Since then, my sewing 'skills' have been confined to sewing on the odd button and trying to mend an article of clothing that I really like, but only if I am really bored. God forbid dementia sets in, and I forget how much I hate needlework.

Scrapbooks

Rating: 1 per cent. But only if I could compile a scrapbook of interesting pictures I have collected of storm drains (i.e. none).

Apparently, yes, these are popular and something I thought had disappeared from my life at the age of seven. Trying to get an old person to do a scrapbook sounds a bit patronizing to me, but each to her own, I suppose, and I'm sure some people really do like it (she said unconvincingly).

Painting

Rating: 25 per cent (if it's walls).

I perked up a bit when I saw painting in a list of things older people might like doing, until I realized it was the artistic pursuit, not slapping on a sickly luminous Farrow & Ball orange colour called 'Shades of Donald'. I do envy people who are artistic, but I am most definitely not one of them. I don't mind trawling through a gallery from time to time, but have to say, certain exhibitions have made me lose the will to live – not a good idea when you're heading towards the age of art gallery visits.

Bowls

Rating: –100 per cent

This game/sport, whatever it is, is very closely tied to older people, all dressed in white with their straw hats on, indulging in what must be the gentlest of exertion, apart from picking up the ball. I do remember it being played in the village where I spent many years at the local primary school in Benenden and thinking it looked very boring then. All the participants looked pristine and ancient. Well, I've never managed pristine. I'm one of those people who attracts random stains when they are least welcome, and I marvel at women who can manage to wear a white suit all day and not end up looking like a chef whose chocolate pudding exploded down their front. And as for ancient, I don't think I'll be very good at that at all.

Jigsaws

Rating: 0 per cent. Just no.

I often used to visit my dad in his residential home and see a few people hunched over tables staring intently at half-completed pictures of horses or rural scenes. My dad never did jigsaws, probably because there weren't any of scaffolding.

I wish I liked doing jigsaws, because they take bloody ages and sometimes mindless is the place you want to be and you can't listen to *Thought for the Day* on Radio 4 all the time. And if I was stuck in a residential facility, or anywhere I didn't like, I would want something to focus on for hours. Some people absolutely love them. Apparently, these people are called 'dissectologists' and they are 'detail orientated, patient and enjoy creating order out of chaos'. I am unfortunately the polar opposite of all those adjectives, so will not even be trying to like jigsaws in the future. If I enjoyed creating order out of chaos my house would look quite nice. I don't and it doesn't.

The New Dawn

So far, I have detailed some of the very traditional pursuits that older people have taken up over the centuries, but, praise be, the very narrow options older women have always had have broadened over the years into an array of choices outside the domestic sphere. Hooray! I doubt very much that throughout their younger lives women have had the time to indulge in womanly pursuits or, like me, they didn't want to. Due to the women's movement, the lives of most women in this country have changed beyond recognition over the past hundred years and given us a degree of independence, much to the delight of Andrew Tate et al., meaning those of us who aren't very ladylike can perhaps branch out a bit, put down the bed socks we weren't knitting, or the embroidery we weren't doing, and head for the erstwhile men-only pursuits. I hope I am speaking for a few people here. I realize that lots of women and some men probably love this sort of pastime but I really don't, so what are the other available hobbies that might attract the 'unfeminine' woman and the man who doesn't like football?

Doing Nothing in Particular

Rating: 90 per cent. Yes, please.

I will start with this as it is often frowned upon. I can spend entire days just pissing about doing very little of any note and I've practised that a lot.

Having Writer's Block

Um . . .

Protests

Rating: 5 per cent. Not averse to the idea, just the practicalities (like nearest toilet: 4 miles).

One thing many older people (and a substantial percentage of them are older women) are getting involved in is protesting. This is on behalf of organizations like the now defunct Just Stop Oil, whose method of protest favours disruption of the day-to-day activities of people, so this can involve chaining yourself to something (echoes of the Suffragettes) or lying down en masse to block roads. One bonus of this is the 'lying down' bit, although you might have forgotten your yoga mat and laid down on a bit of dog shit. So, swings and roundabouts. However, these protests have succeeded in making motorists so angry, it's not the most comfortable environment to have a quick nap in, or indeed the most successful way of getting a message across without completely pissing people off.

Other career opportunities you seem to have with Just Stop Oil are lobbing soup at famous paintings, which are invariably protected by a screen anyway, and I can't think of many older people, me included, who would agree to waste a tin of Heinz tomato soup in that way. Pardon shameless cliché.

Online Shenanigans

Rating: 0.0017 per cent

The world is a very divided place today, and because of the immediacy of communication, we are occasionally subjected to news AS IT IS HAPPENING with no opportunity to filter stuff personally or understand what we are seeing. It is then played on a loop until people get so sick of it, the producer feels obliged to put out a story about a kitten and a lamb who are best friends. This has resulted in many people not bothering with news at all, or watching news through the filter of a politically biased organization, which I think is dangerous, because you start getting news pre-filtered through someone else's opinions, like TikTok for the young person who has a concentration span of –0.005 of a second. Many older people do not ever get online, which is a shame because there are some lovely pictures of kittens on there.

I often think it must be so weird for people in their eighties and nineties who as teenagers in the 1950s barely got a look at anything controversial, so controlled was the news then. In some ways it's probably a blessing that they are not social-media literate, as the shock of seeing some of the hideousness online would make your hair stand on end, let alone turn it white overnight.

Wild Swimming

Rating: 80 per cent with about 47 caveats.

I actually used to love wild swimming. These days, not quite so much. As a kid I would swim in the sea and in rivers whenever I got the chance and really enjoyed it. I don't suppose you'd be surprised to hear that the sea and rivers aren't quite as palatable as they once were, given that, as I have mentioned elsewhere, there are some unwelcome little parcels floating about.

A couple of things put me off about the sea in the UK before that, one of them being the lack of transparency. At one point, I must have been about six at the time, my grandad (the big one) dived off a breakwater head-first into a rock he hadn't spotted under the surface. He got out of the water looking very much the worse for wear, and nevertheless gave us all the very helpful warning never to try that. And, judging our dad's expression to mean 'Don't you dare laugh', we managed not to.

Swimming in lakes is lovely too, but all around the edges can be quite boggy and I've found myself stuck in the mud on more than one occasion. Note to self: do not go swimming in a lake on your own (highly unlikely anyway). I was once taking part in a sponsored swim along the coast in Sussex and chatting away to a friend. A bloke on the shore shouted, 'Shut your mouth!' at me. 'Rude!' I called out. 'No,' he retorted, 'you're coming up to the sewage pipe.'

Mass Clean-ups

Rating: 15 per cent. Very useful if not restful.

No, not your bedroom. These clean-ups tend to address littering in beauty spots, and as we know from the mountainous piles of rubbish hiding just off motorways, it's quite a common hobby these days. I'd rather do this than sewing, so there's a possibility it might happen. I was once in a car with another comic, and we were driving through beautiful countryside on a lovely day to a show in the middle of nowhere. He turned to me and said, 'I love the countryside,' while almost simultaneously chucking an empty Coke can out of the window. I wanted to chuck him out too.

So, in summary, it looks like I will be eschewing using the word 'eschewing' more than twice in this book and along with that I'll be busy doing nothing, interspersed with this and that. I wonder if I've made that clear enough.

HOW TO SURVIVE RETIREMENT

1. Don't retire then you don't need to survive it. I wouldn't recommend trying it the other way round.
2. Lower your expectations lower than you ever thought it was possible to lower them, then lower them a bit more. Then you won't be disappointed at all by retirement.
3. Invent a new hobby specifically tailored to you, like sewing all your old jumpers together to make curtains.
4. Try not to think of yourself as 'silver' anything, because you are 'Gold! Always believe in your soul, you've got the power to know you're indestructible!' (apologies to Spandau Ballet). Sing this every time you are invited to Silver Yoga or Silver Limping-Round-The-Park.
5. Sign up for lots of drug trials and eventually you might find something that makes you feel really great.
6. Moan to anyone who will listen about the price of fish and see if they get the joke.

7. Get a quad bike, a big hat and goggles and get your best friend to do the same. Then you can have races round the park.
8. Keep a journal about the three most boring things you do every day and try to make it sound as exciting as you can.
9. Give yourself a point for everything you do in a day that's useful and when you get to 10 points, award yourself a day off to do things of no value whatsoever.
10. On Sundays only eat mini eggs (or a chocolate of your choice).

CHAPTER FIFTEEN

My Name is Jo!

The idea of being 'looked after' for any length of time fills me with horror.

Is it a good idea to get things in place in your head, ready for when you are an old and possibly helpless person not wanting to be at the mercy of other people and not near to an open window to dive out of? Not that I'd get it right, I was always a bit useless at diving. I was once showing off in a swimming pool to some little kids I was looking after and one of them asked me about diving, so I said I'd show them, got in the position, perfect dive in and realized within a split second I was in the shallow end. Too late! My face hit the bottom of the pool, teeth went through my face just above my top lip, and I came up out of the pool surrounded by red. Quite a few of the children clapped as they obviously thought that was how you were meant to do it. I was borne straight off to A&E where they told me my face was too swollen to use an anaesthetic, so I was forced to go through the stitching process without any. That hurt quite a lot and over the next few weeks I either had to go out with my hand over my mouth as if I was constantly surprised or not go out at all. I did think of going out with a headscarf folded across my face in a triangle but decided I either looked utterly ridiculous or like I was on my way to rob a bank. Yes, I am not a very sensible person.

So, if you do end up spending a very long time in hospital or in a residential facility, how do you claw back some independence and fun? I'm not talking pyjamas with massive pockets so you can hide chocolate in them, but rather being prepared for the way in which people might treat you.

If you're in a residential place which is short-staffed and busy, there are times people are generally going to have to treat you as everywoman/everyman and their approach might be very different from what you're used to. I don't mean being addressed as 'Your Majesty' and fed your favourite dinner every night or anything. In many people's cases, just being addressed by their own name would be a good enough start for them.

And if that is good enough for you as a start, maybe try the following. Firstly, if you get as far as having to endure carers, much as they mean to be kind, and they mostly are, they may treat you as if you're a child and this can be very galling if you're used to being treated as an adult. I know 'endure' is a harsh word – I am not in any way putting carers down, as I know they are overworked and underpaid – but if you possibly can, you want to hang on to every shred of dignity you have left and, from my experience, this is one of the first things to go. I use the word 'endure' because, even if I was being cared for by absolute angels, I would still find it unbearable and would prefer to be off my face on something so I could cope with it. Sadly, I don't think they offer 'getting the patient pissed' in care facilities, apart from the place my dad was in where they seemed to specialize in the patient going unconscious briefly . . .

I am reminded of the three nuns in their eighties who 'ran' away from their residential home in Austria in September 2025 to return to their convent. They had been very happy in the home but were forced to leave because they were the only ones left. They had been guaranteed a place there to live out the rest of their days, but this arrangement was reneged on. The convent was just outside Salzburg, which most ancient old boots will remember is where Sister Maria (aka Julie Andrews) brandished her guitar and made outfits out of curtains.

The nuns were able to re-enter their old convent with the help of some students and a locksmith. Since they left the convent, the stairlift they had been using was removed. (I don't think it was for mischievous or nefarious reasons.) This meant they had to tackle some very steep stairs without help, but one would imagine (them being nuns and all that) someone is watching over them.

What a lovely story, fugitive nuns racing away from a life that made them unhappy. They may now be free of humans 'looking after' them, but many of the rest of us might not be, so let's all gird our loins and make a plan of how to cope in a residential setting.

Escaping, should one feel the need, might not be so easy or romantic.

So, for starters, you might need to keep telling carers your actual name for a bit if you are constantly addressed as 'love', 'darling', 'poppet' or 'sweetheart' and you don't like it. (All of these I have heard in a variety of settings, and although some people may not be bothered by it, I would be.) So at some point, it might be a good idea to have a great big badge made up saying *My name is Jo*. This will enable people to address you by your actual name, which I'm sure we all prefer. I know this is a grumpy approach, but I think one of the issues older people have is being dehumanized and sounding like they have a pet budgie name. Just add an 'ey' onto mine and you're there. While I'm at it, how about some info tattooed on your arm or an embroidered blanket with your likes and dislikes? And I think, at least, it will give carers the opportunity to raise a sardonic eyebrow to their colleagues and think, 'Great, we've got an annoying one.'

I remember visiting my grandma in hospital when she was very old and ill and thinking to myself that, kind as the nurses were, they had no idea of the incredible person she was to everyone that knew and loved her, and it was galling to hear her being treated like an infant. I mean, this was the woman who became a dinner lady (called Mrs Brady, so that was pure poetry) in a secondary school in Herefordshire before she retired. Once, when I went to visit her after she'd retired (she must have been in her eighties by this point), I got out of the car and I was shouted at by a group of teenage boys. 'Fat slag!' – the usual fare. They'd obviously enjoyed my feminist monologues on Channel 4. She had heard the kerfuffle and asked me what had gone on, so I gave her the watered-down version. She told me to wait there and a minute later she returned with one hulking, brutish teenager and one wiry, spotty one, an earlobe of each pinched between two fingers, and instructed them, 'Now say sorry!' Like lambs they mumbled something sounding vaguely like 'sorry', and were escorted from her pristine bungalow with a warning that if there was any more of that, she'd tell their mums. Seemed to put the fear of God up them.

So in order to get a more rounded picture of the individual you have only seen as an elderly lady wearing a flowery dressing gown and sitting quietly in the corner, it would be great to find some ways of telling everyone, staff and residents alike, what sort of person that woman is and what they were like as a younger person. In this day and age with improved technology, there will surely be some holiday videos (yes, only about 18,000 probably) and you could also get their adult children, friends or ex-colleagues to come along and talk about them. I know my daughters would love to come and discuss my brilliant cooking and stylish fashion choices.

Is it inevitable that you will end up being cared for in a residential establishment and feeling unhappy? Not at all, because many people will be satisfied with their treatment. Some of us won't be addressed in this well-meaning but rather childlike way. Maybe some people like it. It's better than being told to shut up and eat your dinner. I think it's good to think about these things now, rather than as you're being escorted in with your suitcase. Like, how the hell do you deal, for example, with being undressed and given a bed bath by people you've never met before? Do they still call them bed baths? Probably not.

I'm not sure if residents are ever asked to fill in a questionnaire about their stay. God knows, there are enough of these infecting every bleeding interaction one has with a service provider and, really, some of those questions are so inane.

Please complete the following questionnaire about your bath:

On a scale of 1 to 10, how would you rate the experience of being lowered into the bath?

10 out of *10,* a right laugh.

On a scale of 1 to 10, how aware of your needs was your carer?

10 out of *10, I* should say, Guv'nor. I ended up sparkling like a scrubbed baby – as clean as clean could be.

You get the picture. I'd always err on the side of positive. If you complain about people who are immediately going to read your thoughts on a questionnaire or as a complaint, it's probably prudent to be positive unless your lungs are already full of water and you've got scrubbing brush burns on your bum.

It's a very common situation for older people in hospital, but it sounds like a horror film to me.

I've been in some places where people's personal possessions seem to have drifted away from them and are available for general distribution, so you've got Mavis's nightie on and Stan's socks on your feet and although you'd rather have something on than nothing, it's another tiny dehumanizing step.

Perhaps it's also a good idea to write out a list of dos and don'ts well in advance of anything happening in the sudden illness scenario, because in this situation people might forget to ask you.

Hair. Polite instruction: Please don't give me a perm or a weird hat (unless it's a top hat with 'Chocolate please' on it). Who needs to worry about calories at this stage of life?

Teeth. If I have false teeth by then, if they even exist any more, please tape them on top of my hat so I don't lose them.

Food. Anything except what's on the two very long lists I have written on the wall.

Clothes. Anything black and baggy (including pants), definitely no pink and no slippers with flowers on them, ditto curtains.

Hopefully that will be a help!

CHAPTER SIXTEEN

The Last Resort

One of my favourite quotes comes from a film called *Sir Henry at Rawlinson End*, a completely bonkers film about an eccentric alcoholic aristocrat who is trying to exorcise the ghost of his brother by supplying it with some replacement trousers (long story). He is looked after by a carer-cum-butler-cum-irritation called Scrotum the Wrinkled Retainer. It was originally serialised on Radio 1 by the eccentric musician Vivian Stanshall on the *John Peel Show* and it is a hoot.

During the film, Sir Henry is heard to roar, 'I don't know what I want, but I want it and I want it now!'

This quote sums up the essence of human nature for me. I think in so many circumstances we know we need *something* but we can't put our finger on what it is or how to get it. I think when most of us imagine ending up in a care home, it fills us with dread because of the largely tangential relationships some of us have had with care homes in the past when we've visited relatives, or we fear the clichés about their potential grimness, which we're not even sure are real.

So, I'm going to think about how to thrive and survive in a care home. (Not literally, *metaphorically*, by the way.)

One positive way of looking at going into a care home is the difference it could make for many older people who may have been living alone for a while and not coping, even with relatives visiting regularly; or perhaps their carers are just not coming regularly enough or, on the other hand, their relatives and carers come often enough, but they just don't like them. So, to a great extent, if you get the right care home, it can become a sanctuary where you can have your own space and yet not be called upon to keep the place clean and prepare meals, plus you can make friends and be entertained as and when you feel like it. Of course, if you are in an advanced state of dementia, and who knows what that feels like until it happens to you, it's going to be tricky, which is why you need to become a scout temporarily and 'Be prepared!'

The main problem is that there are so many variables and people are all different, even though 'old people' tend to be viewed as all roughly the same, much more so than any other generation.

How to Be Prepared

My preferred method of preparing for the future is burying my head in the sand and hoping things will be fine. I'm not sure this is the most successful method in this case. I'm not saying you should tour the country in an open-top bus visiting every care home you can and seeing which one does the best roast potatoes or how big the telly in your room would be, but it might be a good idea to be aware of the possibilities and how much you're going to have to shell out for them if you are anywhere near in a position to do so, which of course many people are not.

Whether or not things will change and the care system will be magically sorted out by the time you need it is impossible to predict, so best not to ignore it completely and err on the side of 'probably not'. I realize this is not a good start on the optimism front, but a few people will know right from the off that they're staying put at home and that's that. Others may be prepared to compromise, but, let's face it, the older you get, ironically, the less likely that is to happen, because with age comes a very strong sense of I-Know-What-I-Like, so work on that in case they haven't got your favourite brand of custard creams or the vintage champagne you like on your cornflakes.

For those of us who are ambivalent about the possibility of going into a care home, it's going to be very different, but having worked in many different care settings over the years, I feel like I've gleaned the following life lessons . . .

All care homes seem the same, but they're not. So, you need to get a vague idea of what you want beforehand, in case you find yourself with any kind of choice. Of course, the day-to-day routine is similar in most – they can be a little one-size-fits-all – so you're not going to find something that's perfect for you. Therefore, you need to decide on a list of things you probably won't compromise on (of no more than maybe five items . . . Don't go down the route of 'But twenty-seven isn't that many!'). And I'm not talking a Georgian four-poster bed and a view of the Sphinx here, but, more generally, 'being comfortable' and 'having a window' sort of level. Don't expect to bring your collection of 173 Royal Doulton teapots either.

Generally, I would hope that the care home doesn't remind me of a Dickens novel in any way. Dickens was a genius, but the conditions in those days weren't. When I was much younger, I worked in two very contrasting residential homes for adults with learning disabilities, and the first one seemed to be modelled on the Dickensian ethos of Oliver Twist's early life. The men who lived there had their trouser pockets sewn up, for example, (I'll leave the reason for that to your imagination) and tea came in a huge teapot: tea leaves, milk and sugar all slung in together, yuk. Added to this, there was a somewhat menacing atmosphere. Some things just weren't right. I made a complaint to the boss, and he suggested I leave. That's how they did things in the early 1970s, folks! Thankfully, these sorts of places are a thing of the past.

Personally, I'd lean more towards the second residential place I worked in. It was modern in comparison, light, welcoming and fun. Every Friday night we pulled all the furniture back, put very loud music on and everyone danced like dervishes to cheerful songs like 'Thank You for the Music' by Abba.

I was learning how to drive at the time, and my brother Bill would pick me up after work in his tiny little bright-orange car, and I would take the wheel and drive us home. On the very first occasion, everyone came out to wish me luck and see me off. I got in, started the engine, then panicked massively and instead of driving in a graceful arc round the ornamental flower garden, ploughed straight across it. All I could see in the mirror were thirty people clapping, cheering and pissing themselves laughing. Happy days.

I should just add here that approximately 70 per cent of people in residential care for the elderly have some form of dementia or memory issues, so I'll try to take that into account as we head onwards.

The Intellectual Side

Much as we would all like our care home to be like *The Thursday Murder Club*, I think it's probably highly unlikely. But that doesn't mean you can't try to keep the old brain ticking over as much as you are able. I do think people make enemies in a place where they are kind of all lumped together and don't have any choice, so maybe there will be a couple of nice palatable murders to solve which could be something of a hobby, I suppose. Perhaps it is time now for me to explore how I might keep myself occupied if I do end up in residential care . . .

Bugs

Not the kind you might find in your bed, although I did have an issue when I was about 13 with scabies. (Yes, I can visualize your expressions.) This was from staying at someone's house occasionally during the week, rather than making a 50-mile round trip daily to and from school. Unfortunately, over six months it got really, really bad, because our family GP didn't seem to be able to work out what it was, and by the time a dermatologist had diagnosed it (in about half a second, I might add), I was covered from head to foot with it and it was decided I needed to be residential in order for some concentrated regular treatment over three weeks. And that is how I ended up as a patient in my first nursing home in Hove (epicentre of the retired population) on the south coast. I can barely remember anything about it apart from being painted from head to foot twice a day with this evil-smelling concoction and seeing nothing but old people when I ventured out of my room. Anyway, the treatment did the trick and with relief I bade farewell to the place.

That is all by the by. The sort of bugs I'd like to have if I was in a residential place are the secret listening type. I'd plant them around the building and spend all day listening to people's conversations. I know that's not a very ethical thing to do, but I couldn't resist hearing what they all had to say about us, the residents, and what's really going on in the place. It's so rare any of us truly gets to hear what other people think of us and, quite honestly, I would find it fascinating – despite having religiously ignored reviews for the last forty years.

Socializing

Be honest, from the kick-off, you're not going to get on with everyone. It's like staying in hospital, except permanent, with far fewer beds and the added bonus of individual rooms. If you can find one person you like and that you can have a laugh with, that'll do for starters.

I'd be more worried that people wouldn't get on with

me. I wasn't exactly one of the popular girls at school. And by 'popular girl' I mean 'popular/mean girl' who rules the group with a rod of sarcasm and flicky hair. 'Mean' in this context is unpleasant rather than unforthcoming with their pocket money, and something which crossed the Atlantic from the US well after my school days. I wonder if there is such a thing as an 85-year-old mean girl. I'm looking forward to finding out.

Ingratiating Myself With the Staff

I would also try to get along as best I can with all the staff. You're not leaving at the end of the day, unless you're a fan of *The Great Escape*. (A film that used to be on EVERY CHRISTMAS when I was a child, so I pretty much know the entire script back to front. I quite fancy trying to escape just for the hell of it and favour the 'Being Wheeled Out in a Laundry Basket' method.)

Perhaps it would be a good idea to pinpoint the member of staff you like best and try to get them on your side as an ally, so that if you need anything you can rely on them to be helpful and they will be able to advocate for you, should you be caught nicking someone else's slippers or accidentally weeing on their new copy of *The Lady* (a magazine not for the likes of me). Bribery, flattery, gifts – whatever it takes, it's always good to have someone in your corner.

I would suggest not making too many demands on the staff's time, being polite and not constantly pressing the buzzer in your room, whacking the gong or just screeching as loud as you can. (Yes, I'm a bit hazy on details of how it all works in accommodation for the elderly.)

Take a Pet

Even if dogs, cats and domesticated rodents aren't allowed, that won't stop me taking some sort of pet. Personally, I'm leaning towards a snail. (Yes, that's part of my plan to keep me cheery. Easy to feed, even easier to chase . . .)

Exercise

Older people in residential care accommodation are also encouraged to stay active. Well, I certainly won't be taking any notice of that particularly pointless exhortation.

And Finally, Tattoos!

No, not the military ones that so delight tourists in Edinburgh and feature a lot of people in kilts marching up and down for hours and hours, but the ones that are etched on your skin forever unless you fork out a shedload of money to have them removed. I have one tiny tattoo on the inside of my arm, so I think I could really go to town if I was in a residential home for the elderly and leave some messages all over myself for various people I know, or perhaps just some one-liners for anyone that needed a laugh.

The Dignity Side of Things . . .

One thing that can disappear double-quick when you move into a place for the elderly is your dignity. Many people will not be able to remain continent, for example, and to me the idea of being dressed, changed or bathed by someone I don't know is perhaps the most prominent horror in my mind, beside the fact that it must be weird to have an intimate relationship of that sort with a passing carer. (See 'Bugs' above for the first serious infringement of my dignity.)

I would like to banish that word 'incontinence' as it tends only to be applied to older people. Come on, we all piss ourselves from time to time. I did, at a bus stop when I was 13. We were waiting for the bus and someone really made me laugh and I couldn't help myself . . . just as the bus arrived too.

Indignity follows us throughout our lives. I also lost a lot more dignity many years ago when my brother Bill turned up at a gig I did in Hastings, whisked Jeff (the other comedian), John (our tour manager) and me off to a hotel and *made* us drink a lot of crème de menthe. After this horror, Jeff and John fell asleep, whereas I, wandering about in the dark looking for the toilet, walked out of the room without any clothes on and the door of my room banged loudly behind me. I was discovered by the night porter and taken back to my room . . . the horror! He told me all this the next morning, completely straight-faced and rather miserable-looking, and as he was the spitting image of Scrotum the Wrinkled Retainer it was one of the most surreal encounters of my life. But considering I couldn't remember any of it, and I think he said he'd dealt with much worse, it wasn't quite as shameful as it could have been. We were so hung-over, Jeff, John and I went into the chemist to get soluble something-or-other, and the pharmacist took one look at us and went and fetched some water and three glasses and made us drink the concoction straight away. We then went to do another show in Basingstoke and I had to invest all my energy into standing very still in front of the mic trying not to projectile vomit for an hour.

Back to the plot . . .

All of this is to say, it's easy to forget the indignity that follows us through our lives.

I think I would take some clothes into the home with me and make sure that they couldn't *possibly* belong to anyone else, because they were so hideous. There's no doubt that clothes can go missing in homes for the elderly, and you don't want to run the risk of wearing some old bloke's pants, so the advice is to label everything with a permanent marker or sew name labels onto everything. Hmm, what does that sound like? Yep, school. I'll probably get some big baggy T-shirts with my name across in huge letters, and some choice swear words at the bottom, so no one else would ever be seen dead in them, pardon the expression.

So, my main takeaway from this chapter on how to survive a residential home is:

Vegetable curry, pilau rice and naan bread. Or 'nan' bread, as I prefer it to be called. Apologies to the young people.

CHAPTER SEVENTEEN
Grave Expectations

Even though most of us know that there are no such thing as ghosts, and that hardly any evil murderers lurk in graveyards these days, very few of us would agree to have an overnight stay in a graveyard alone. I think that's probably because we have all been programmed over the years to believe they are places of evil, despite them being attached to churches, which are supposed to be the polar opposite of evil. Although the institution of the church has constantly updated itself and made changes that would have been unimaginable even thirty years ago, in my head, graveyards and cemeteries have stayed in the realms of the past like medieval theme parks where evil spirits lurk and terror and murder await.

So how did this happen? Well, children, a long time ago, when I was probably about five years old, I watched the opening of the black-and-white film of *Great Expectations*. This is many people's favourite Charles Dickens novel and begins with young Pip terrified out of his wits by a murderous escaped criminal in a graveyard at dusk. This scene has walked through my dreams in one form or another ever since, featuring shaven-headed monstrosities lurking about behind gravestones as the light gradually fades towards night. Chuck in some ghosts, and a cheery group of the undead (otherwise known as 'The Women's Institute') and you have the traditional picture of what also constituted the horror genre in the UK in the 1960s. Yes, that was enough to scare us wimps. We were not in need of chainsaws, human centipedes or any of the more recent common horror tropes. A simple graveyard did the trick.

To chug onwards aboard the cliché train, picture if you will: rain, weeping relatives holding umbrellas, an emaciated priest about seven feet tall, a scruffy gravedigger with a roll-up stuck to his lip, and you have your archetypal funeral cast.

We also need to give the starring role to the colour black here. It was a rule unbroken for centuries that everyone who attended a funeral wore black, the only funeral-savvy shade that would be tolerated in that setting by any right-minded sad person.

Black: the enemy of joy and friend of the fat person. I realized over the years that it was the colour for me. As well as being able to relax about choosing clothes and harking back to my mother's anodyne palette of dullish colours, wardrobe-wise, it made my life so much easier.

And now that I have decided to pretty much wear black all the time I can properly breathe out, literally, instead of fighting against friends, family and wardrobe people. I remember one of my older relatives saying to me, 'But you'd look so pretty in pink or light blue.' For fuck's sake, I've never looked 'pretty' in anything, nor would I want to. I'm not a 'pretty' sort of person. Surely that word should be reserved for the under tens. I'll stop ranting. It's interesting though, most of my friends when we meet up will comment on what another friend is wearing, 'Is it new? Love the sleeves . . .' etc., etc. At this point I go into a temporary coma until they have finished, and I can rejoin the conversation.

When I was at primary school, the Church of England was far less prescriptive than the Catholic church, so I didn't have the fear of God and/or the priest hanging over me as a child. The Church of England was also much more liberal and so midnight mass at Christmas, on occasion, morphed into an extension of the pub for some people, who belted out the carols with the same gusto they would apply to rugby songs. This is not and never has been the case for funerals. They ARE NOT social events first and foremost and unless the poor deceased was a very young person, they tend to be attended mainly by family and assorted old people.

In the old days the structure of a funeral was similar everywhere for Christians. Normally, there would be a couple of hymns that were considered suitable, of the 'Abide with Me' variety. 'Abide with Me' is my favourite hymn and I think is generally considered *the* funeral hymn to include. However, it is not really considered to be suitable for other types of religious services, as I found out when discussing my wedding service with a vicar in Ludlow where I got married. (You might be wondering, 'Why is someone like you getting married in church?' Remember what I just said about the Church of England?).

Anyway, the vicar did try to talk me out of my favourite hymn, but I begged and so he caved in and agreed to include it. As I had had some success with my first choice, I thought I'd have another crack, because my second favourite hymn is 'For Those in Peril on the Sea'.

Well, sadly, the line was drawn at that.

Right, back to funerals.

Funerals are conducted in church by vicars and the like, and in non-consecrated areas by someone who is known as a 'celebrant'. Considering King Henry VIII invented the Church of England so he could divorce his first wife without too much hassle (not to mention kill off a couple more) and not get into too much trouble, there is a fairly liberal attitude towards attendance. So, theoretically, you could never have set foot in a church before, but you could still get married in one. (Yep, that's me! I think you may have to have been baptized in a church to be married in one, but am somewhat hazy on the details.) And the same goes for being seen out of this world, as it were. So, it's highly unlikely that any person conducting a funeral will have known your relative very well, and therefore, everything they say will have been fed to them by a relative or partner. This unfortunately means that the information can be quite skewed, and I would imagine many a relative has fumed silently in the congregation as they hear Mr Arsehole described as Mr Charming. So, occasionally, the person whose life is being celebrated will not be recognizable to many members of the congregation.

This has happened to me once or twice, and I felt a very strong urge to heckle. Heckling at funerals is frowned upon, which I think is a shame if some important detail about that person is completely wrong. So, unless the interruption is of the drunken comedy heckler variety, I do think the congregation should be encouraged to interject in an 'Objection, Your Honour' kind of way. Yes, I realize that could extend the funeral to several days, but families may have a very different view of an individual member which contrasts with long-standing friends and maybe the occasional interruption would lighten the mood.

My mum's funeral was in the open air in a beautiful rural setting and my brother and I managed it between us. There were a lot of my mum's very close friends there and the floor was thrown open to anyone that wanted to say anything. A lot of people did say something, and it was a real mixture of funny, sad, awkward, long, short, silly and beautiful, which is a lot more than can be said for some stilted ceremonies. There is, after all, going to be plenty of time for crying afterwards in whichever setting you choose. I am not a good public crier, because our family was at the stiffest end of the 'stiff upper lip' continuum.

Many funerals today can be much more relaxed and tailored towards the deceased person, because people don't do what they're told by the church any more. I was asked to compile a list of my brother Bill's favourite songs that could be played before and after his funeral and very inappropriately included a song he loved called 'Disco Inferno', not for a minute relating it to the fact that we would be at a crematorium. Thankfully, this was spotted by a member of the family and removed from the list, although I know Bill would have thought it was absolutely hilarious.

Funerals today can be a mix of the contemporary and traditional as we make the transition from hundreds of years of very traditional funerals to those in which mourners have far more choice about how they use ever-changing modern tech to conduct the celebration in the way they want to. Whereas before one could maybe have a photograph of someone on an easel, now it is possible, I would imagine, to show some video footage, although I wonder if certain attendees would find that too difficult to deal with. I suspect it will be avatars next (she said, appearing to possess more knowledge than she actually has).

It's obviously hard to juggle priorities because of the age range of those attending a funeral. For example, if you think that a controversial stand-up comic is a great idea at you grandad's send-off, maybe just run it past others first.

I think both my brothers would have liked some stand-up comedy at their funerals. (Not me doing it, I hasten to add!) I did speak at their funerals, and somehow at my little brother Matt's funeral, I spoke German. Although I got German O level I was not nearly fluent enough to manage it, so asked the husband of a friend of mine to translate a speech I had written in English into German, and it did cross my mind that he could have written anything, but he was a lovely, serious kind of guy, so I knew I was on safe ground. Not so, however, when I was having a chat some years before with Matt's father-in-law after we'd been for quite a long walk in the forest. Helmut asked me if I'd enjoyed the walk. Remember my German is only mildly OK . . . so I thought I'd said, 'Yes, lovely, but my feet hurt.' What I actually said was, 'Yes, lovely, but my cunt (sorry, c***) hurts.' No wonder he looked like he was about to faint.

We do like to remember those we have loved with something tangible and visible, and for that reason, I suppose, gravestones were invented. They are there to identify who's in there, but also to give people a chance to give instructions about what they want written about themselves. I suppose leaving it to chance is risky.

Spike Milligan, the legendary comedian, has the words 'I told you I was ill' on his gravestone. Although to get the diocese to agree to it these words are written in Gaelic.

If what you want to say on your headstone is important to you, it's probably best to let your relatives know and I'm pretty certain you can have absolutely anything you want these days in plain old English. So, we are in something of a transitional period as far as funerals are concerned. Though I suspect headstones may be a thing of the past as graveyards are sold off to fund the vicar's ketamine habit.

I imagine in the not-too-distant future there might be avatars of people who could be hailed at the push of a button and you could have a chat with them. Me, I'd rather just have a sentence on a mossy bit of stone.

Acceptable phrases for me would be:

'I forgot to turn my electric blanket off.'
'Stop doing that.'
'I'm a celebrity, get me out of here!'
'Can someone get me some chocolate, please.'
'Ow!'
Etc., etc.

Statues are an interesting concept too, given that

most of them don't look anything like the person they're modelled on. These days, crowdfunding ensures that a lot of people who would not have been considered deserving enough end up being crowdfunded into a statue, even though their auntie Doris might end up looking more like Auntie Boris.

Still, if having a statue of yourself is your thing, you can at least start saving now. And I'd much rather see someone like Terry Jones from Monty Python on a plinth than George The Something.

There is something about the general décor at a funeral director's. Do they have to look like a cross between a prison cell and a cut-price IKEA? So drab! So depressing! So funereal! Yes, yes, I know they're meant to be, but if you saw a picture and were asked what service they offered, you would always get it right. How about some comfy chairs or a bit of colour? How about some music? It doesn't have to be 'Happy Talk' by Captain Sensible. I doubt anyone's going to complain. Let's get some flamboyance going!

It's getting a bit miserable, isn't it? Let's get something more positive into the mix. An attempt at cheerfulness is happening in Germany where for a while there have been cemetery cafés, so that if you go to visit someone's grave, you can have coffee or a bun while you're at it. I do rather like this idea, because it adds a new aspect to places like cemeteries and graveyards that we normally tend to consider depressing, and hopefully encourages people to be more positive about the place where their loved one is. And if people hate going there with their family they can always decamp to the café after a decent amount of time, normally about fifteen seconds in the case of a child.

Many people choose, once their loved one is cremated, to scatter their ashes in a place that they loved, like a football ground or in some picturesque beauty spot. That's not for their benefit, though, is it? Apparently, there is a danger of too many people flocking to beauty spots to scatter the ashes. Tussocks may become little hills which may become mountains. Fair enough, I exaggerate, but do you really want grandad to become a small hillock with a load of other randomly scattered individuals? (Not random to their families, I hasten to add.)

I'm not sure I realized before some family ashes came into my possession after being looked after by someone else for six years (long story) that there's quite so much of the stuff. Scattering would take an age if you didn't want to leave any evidence of your visit to Buckingham Palace.

I did think, with my dad's ashes, that having taken them out for the day to spread them far and wide and after a couple of random scatters, that the grass began to look a bit grey and, well, 'ashy'. So, I beat a retreat home and resolved to put them in the garden and plant a tree, but when I perused the internet, I discovered that if you put more than a very small amount when planting them around the base of a tree, you will kill the tree. Back to square one.

Well, in the olden days the choice was pretty much an urn or nothing. These days, however, ashes can become jewellery; for example, diamonds.

'Matilda! Is that a ring you're wearing?'

'Yes! I have just got engaged!'

'What a gorgeous ring.'

'It's gold and Grandma.'

You can also put your loved one's ashes in a vinyl record. Maybe this is the time for me to do the 'Disco Inferno' thing!

I'm not sure about putting a loved one into a firework. Perhaps if you didn't like them very much? I once did a show in Guildford with my mate Jeff Green, and it just happened to be 5 November, so we bought a biggish rocket on the way to the show and put it in an upright bottle and lit it. Unfortunately, at the last minute the bottle toppled over, and the rocket shot out and exploded underneath a caravan near the stage door. In one of the most memorable and surreal moments of my life, the door opened almost immediately and a very angry children's clown in full regalia appeared and remonstrated with us in the filthiest, sweariest way you could imagine. Presumably, not the sort of things he shouted in his shows. We apologized profusely whilst attempting our hardest not to guffaw.

Sorry, one more firework story: a friend of mine who is Danish was in Copenhagen for a firework celebration which involved some VIPs and assorted minor royals standing on a balcony. Someone set off a rocket in a nearby garden from its position in a bottle. They hadn't realized the bottle still had some water in it which had frozen solid, so when the firework took off, it carried the bottle with it and headed straight for the balcony. The people in the firing line managed to duck and it smashed right through an ornate window behind them. Now that's what I call a firework display. However, I am not suggesting you attempt a re-creation of this at your great-aunt Madge's funeral.

By far the weirdest and grandest thing you can do with ashes is create a memorial reef which will weave itself into the eco system of the sea. What eco system? Maybe just go for an urn?

MY FUNERAL PLAN

Apparently only 5 per cent of people have a funeral plan. In many ways, I'm not surprised and it makes me feel a lot better. It's not the first thing you put on your to-do list when you hit 70 or feel a bit of a sniffle coming on, is it? And most of us are not global stars or royals who need to have a very carefully curated funeral with the streets lined with crowds and police on tap.

And who wants to be thinking about that anyway? We have a proud tradition in this country of not wanting to think about *anything like that.* So, unless you have either a very organized approach to everything or a funeral fetish, just carry on being in denial. As Freud said, this defence mechanism - which rejects the reality of unpleasant facts and protects you from anxiety - can be destructive in the long term. I think most of us would rather take that risk.

Also, you'll never know if your family listened to your wishes for the ceremony, unless you believe you'll be on some sort of celestial viewing platform with a checklist. I would be part of that 5 per cent but given that I think crying in public is wrong for me, they can all wait until they get home to cry. My kind of funeral would be mercifully short, unstructured and would include many non-funereal touches.

Venue and catering

I do quite like churches but wouldn't particularly want to have an entire ceremony in one. My compromise: everyone could walk *through* the church, so those amongst the group who are religious don't feel hard-done-by, and then head straight out the back exit. On arriving outside the church, there would be big buckets of sweets, doughnuts and cheese. A woman with a big tea urn will hand out cups of tea or shots of vodka or both together.

Celebrant

If possible a younger comedian with a graveyard sense of humour (taking applications).

Music

After a short sermon, I would like everyone to sing a song together, because unless you attend a proper church service, no one actually gets to sing and ends up listening to pieces of music instead, and a good old chorus of something rousing and easy to sing will cheer everyone up. How about something like 'Old MacDonald Had a Farm'? How often is it that adults get to make pig noises in public? I think most people would have a laugh, and quite honestly, that's what you need more of at my kind of funeral.

After-party

The infuriating thing about parties for me is that you don't really get much of an opportunity to talk to the people you *want* to talk to and I always end up getting flattened against a wall, caught in a continuous verbal volley for what seems like days. So, I would like this gathering to be carefully choreographed like speed-dating. If you find yourself trapped, a bell will toll and you can shift on to the next person. Perfect.

Gifts

I don't think it's the done thing to provide the equivalent of party bags after a funeral. Normally you get an order of service with a picture on the front. I think a stick of rock with my name through would be an unusual offering and, of course, bearing in mind a lot of older teeth probably wouldn't be up to it, maybe an alternative like a lollipop. Let's be honest, you don't see enough older people enjoying a lollipop these days, especially not at a funeral.

CHAPTER EIGHTEEN

Always Look on the Bright Side of Life

Well, this looks set to be a cheery chapter but let's be honest here, as you age, managing to avoid the loss of a loved one altogether is impossible, unless you were found under a bush as a baby and have made no friends on your travels through life. It seemed to happen to a few Dickens characters but otherwise is quite hard to do. You would have to try very hard to be completely unbearable company in a variety of ways, like eating sugar out of a bowl with a tablespoon, blowing your nose on the curtains, or seeing how long you can go without having a shower.

In the ten years between 2015 and 2025 I lost both of my brothers, both my parents and two out of my three best friends. My mum and dad were both what some people would describe as 'a good age'. Is any age a good age really, unless it's 120 (although Bryan Johnson might be a bit pissed off with that because it's not old enough)? I think the stiff-upper-lip thing makes it difficult to do grief. We were read the Bible at school when I was a kid, and I always remember grief-stricken women tearing at their garments to show how profound their sorrow was. I think if I could have free rein, smashing plates would have been my thing.

When friends and family start to disappear off the radar, if you make it to very old age without a lot of them, life must start to feel lonely. How we deal with loss is very much a personal affair. I have always been a member of the bury-it-very-deep-and-don't-think-about-it brigade, although I'm not sure this is a particularly healthy approach. But who cares at this point? There are several stages of grieving which I remember vaguely from doing a social sciences degree at university, and I always thought they should be a bit more flexible than that.

The stages are:

Denial. I don't think I did this at all. I accepted it immediately, so that's buggered up the order straight away.

Anger. Yep, was doing that from the start and probably beforehand. I was angry with a lot of my brother's friends for not being my brother, for example, but that's not easy to explain, so I didn't announce it.

Bargaining. Who am I supposed to be bargaining with

and what for? Apparently 'bargaining' here is in the sense of 'struggling to find meaning'. Didn't do that. Also, it involves 'reaching out' to others. Apparently 'reaching out' is a polite alternative for 'contact'. Yes, because 'contact' is such a barbaric, filthy word, isn't it? 'I told him if he contacted me again, I'd reach out and smack him one, the philistine.'

Depression. I think 'sadness' might be a better word here, because it seems more appropriate.

Acceptance. Done that already.

I can certainly see that all those components are valid in that order for some people, apart from maybe 'bargaining'. Also, I think I got stuck at the angry stage for far too long. The thing about being angry is you don't have to express it outwardly and a lot of people turn it in on themselves, which many think is what depression is. On the other hand, I love a bit of a controlled seethe. It doesn't hurt anyone and it's very satisfying.

I know this is sacrilegious, but from time to time in this book, I've had a bit of a moan about how sometimes life is more difficult if people recognize you in situations that you'd much rather be anonymous in. It's not a massive deal, and I accept that I need to suck it up, but it's made some situations much more stressful than they needed to be.

Example: Giving birth in hospital and a doctor

from another department appearing and asking for my autograph . . . just totally weird.

I do understand that I am a dinosaur, floundering about in a world in which it's not possible to press the 'privacy, please' button, while many others in my line of work are opening their hearts, minds and private lives for the scrutiny of others. The problem is that social media is a huge, hungry, demanding and unforgiving monster, causing people to virtually turn themselves inside out looking for validity and love, and despite getting a load of support and positive vibes, this is inevitably accompanied by some anonymous vitriolic hate and filth. I realize I have to find a way of dealing with it, but when I was a nurse working in a mental health emergency clinic, we had several very well-known people come through our doors and I would not have dreamed of even acknowledging that I knew who they were, let alone asking for a picture with them. Obviously, no mobile phones existed in those days. We pretty much had two tin cans joined together by a bit of string, sophistication-wise.

However, when one of my brothers was extremely ill and didn't have very long left, I was asked for a selfie, then to do a video call to someone's mum before being told, 'I'm sorry for your loss'. Obviously prematurely. I'm sure my response wasn't particularly polite. Fair enough if I was in a corridor or a lift, but when I was actually in the room with my poor brother, it felt so insensitive. So, I seethed instead. Maybe that should be my motto.

I also began to wish I could carry a supply of morphine or similar around with me. Not *for* me, but for those occasions when my brother was in extreme pain and yet was not allowed his next dose of painkillers until a certain time. Yes, you might say, but the rules must be obeyed. Well, I think there should be a bit more leeway at this stage of a terminally ill person's life. What difference does it make if someone's obviously not going to make it and yet the family must watch them suffer for the sake of ten minutes? I did actually want to push it with the staff and their priorities. I suppose my seething might have come out a bit here. In fact, I should have just said, 'Give him something now, please, and some for me while you're at it.' This was not the case in the local hospice where my brother went to stay soon after that, and he didn't seem to be in pain at all. And yet hospices are having to close, because they are under-funded owing to a series of complex problems. It was the most delightful place. Well, as delightful as a hospice can be in the circumstances.

I was unable to be with either of my parents when they died because they were so far from where my brothers and I lived (not together!). We were relentlessly South of the River, my brother Matt even more so in Germany.

My dad, who wasn't with my mum any more, lived happily in a flat in Herefordshire quite near to her. My mum was always in the centre of things, much more left-wing than me, a council meeting disrupter and local paper column writer. But, as I've said, she was very secretive about her health. I presumed she didn't want to burden us with anything and perhaps confided in her friends, but I'm pretty sure she wasn't doing that either.

When people reach a certain age, death is less of a shock, but you still want to be there with them. Sadly, for my mum, she became ill during one of the Covid lockdowns and we were not permitted to see her. She insisted that she didn't want my brother Bill and I to drive up and see her at her flat because we'd only be allowed to stand outside in the garden and she didn't feel that minimal degree of contact justified a four-hour drive.

She had told me before that she dreaded being in hospital and being 'looked after' because she was aware of the phenomenon that all older people tend to get treated in the same way by carers. When she was admitted to hospital in the middle of the night, we were still not allowed to go and see her, so I was reduced to long phone calls during which I could hear the hubbub of the ward in the background and various staff speaking to her from time to time.

Unfortunately, these interactions were extremely difficult to listen to as most of the time she was spoken to in a high-pitched voice as if she was a child, and these conversations varied between 'Are you all right, dear?' type interactions, to those remorselessly cheerful, 'How are you doing, young lady?' sort of comments, both of which I knew she would hate. This attitude has always been the case, I think, and comes from a good place, but just doesn't distinguish between patients, in a way that doesn't happen quite so much when people are younger. It is assumed that everyone of a certain age is intellectually challenged in some way, so the default position comes across as patronizing. Having said that, it is meant kindly, done with the best intentions, but for someone whose cognitive faculties are as sharp as they ever were, it is painful.

The nurses weren't to know, for example, that my mum was an ex-social worker with an acute sense of right and wrong, which ranged through lots of incarnations. I remember one incident in which a group of students were waiting anxiously for some exam results on a Friday afternoon, but were told by the somewhat pompous course leader they would have to wait until Monday as he'd locked them in his office. My mum waited until he'd left the building, broke into his office, found the results and handed them round. Go, Joyce!

One nurse, however, was the daughter of someone my mum knew well and I was able to speak to her sometime later and know that my mum had so appreciated her being around. Like many people, the recent Covid inquiry made me feel for all the other poor people who went through the same thing.

Lumping older people together seems to be inevitable and maybe I am expecting too much, especially during a crisis like Covid, but everyone's mum and dad, with a few exceptions, are very precious to them and it's hard to feel that, much as older people in hospitals should be treated as individuals, it simply does not seem to be possible.

So how do we tackle this?

It's difficult. My mum was insistent she never wanted to go into hospital and even went to the lengths of trying to procure something that would allow her to have control over when she could end her life. However, circumstances took over, and she was unable to have her wishes fulfilled. The current ongoing discussion about euthanasia is a difficult one because feelings run very high on both sides of the debate. Unfortunately, the law is unable to encompass all the subtleties, and even though most of the population is in favour of limited permission, so far, no consensus has been achieved, and I can't help thinking that prolonging life at all costs causes a lot of suffering to a great number of people.

Loneliness

It seems as we age and become more solitary, loneliness can become an issue. According to Age UK, by 2026, 2 million people over the age of 50 will feel lonely. Again,

Covid didn't help, as a lot of people found it difficult to get back to a full life after locking down for so long.

So, what are the reasons people get lonely?

I would suggest that there is a difference between men and women. Some men don't feel the need personally to make much of effort to socialize if they are in a relationship. They are very happy for the women in their lives to make the connections. I've known lots of men like this. (Not in the biblical sense.) Then, if their other half dies first, they find themselves lonely and lacking the requisite social skills or inclination to be able to connect with others in a way that would improve the quality of their lives.

It also works the other way round and many women whose husbands die first will find themselves alone and not sure where to begin on making connections too.

Some people are just too shy to start the process of trying to meet others. Sometimes the rather unhelpful advice of 'join a club' is just too much for them to tackle. I think it can be much harder in a big town or city to combat loneliness. I was brought up in a series of small towns and villages, and especially in villages, people do tend to keep an eye on each other. Joining in can be easier when you at least know people by sight, and you can ask someone to keep an eye on you. Having said that, it's a fine line between 'keeping an eye on' and being downright nosey. And 'nosey neighbours' are a well-known phenomenon, not to mention unscrupulous neighbours who may well be eyeing up your tea-towel collection. You don't want to give a neighbour a key and then suddenly be faced by them opening the door to find you there with just your favourite big girl pants on.

In a large city, it's very easy to be ignored, particularly in London, where 'everyone is horrible', according to one of my aunts. All right, maybe that's a bit extreme, but the good Samaritans are slightly harder to spot in London because everyone tends to try to wear the dogged expression of 'don't mess with me'. Much of London is actually a series of 'villages' where people do know each other and I've lived in a few areas where people keep an eye out for neighbours. Once accommodation started growing towards the sky rather than sideways, I think it became harder to get a sense of your neighbours, and so maybe these are the areas to concentrate on in the future. Once the technophobe generation who cannot be reached online can be included, I think communication might be easier.

It's possible a lot of people have driven away friends by being very unpleasant, unfriendly or downright rude and might not want someone knocking on the door asking if they're OK.

Maybe they just want to be with other unpleasant people, although that might not work as a potential dating column in *The Oldie*.

I think loneliness is common in old age because of the

lumping-together of old people and assuming they will just get on. And God forbid they send a 'young' person round to chat with me regularly. I mean this in a kind way. Sounds like I'm shaping up to be a very grumpy old person. But let's face it, they are a lot more fun.

I think we should perhaps remember too that a lot of people don't really get lonely, so it's probably better to supply them with information and let them make the choice, rather than forcibly bundle them into a minibus and take them on a day out somewhere. Looking at my local area, I see the sort of activities available are guided walks in local parks, yoga, museums and gallery visits. Well, they are all OK, I suppose, apart from yoga and walks in local parks which I've done a fair bit of. Just parks, not yoga (God forbid!). It goes without saying that women do become somewhat invisible as they age, which makes us great shoplifters, drug mules, store detectives and spies. So, here I am moaning about what's available, very unconstructive of me without adding a few of my suggestions.

Here we go then:

1. A friend of mine does supporting artiste work (or 'extra', if you're quite old). They always need old people in a crowd and the money's pretty good. You get fed and you meet people. What could be better? On the downside, they do

quite long days, but then again, if you're a telly watcher, it is pretty rubbish during the day.

2. My mum favoured getting stuck into local council meetings. I'd especially like to go to somewhere Reform is running the council and see how they are getting on, maybe heckle a bit and get chucked out when I'm bored.
3. You could join an environmental protest; you might get an extended lie-down.
4. Stand-up comedy? It's an ever-expanding genre, and you could just do a list of things that piss you off – that would really cheer me up if I went to see a comedian like that.
5. How about drug trials? Medical researchers are always looking for people in all areas of medicine. It's worth a try.
6. Stand-in cover for your local lollipop lady (I don't even know whether this job exists), or there might be a vacancy for full time. Very short hours at least.
7. How about being a steward at a football ground? Even if you don't really like football, it's good fun just to listen to all the swearing, which can be highly imaginative. Then you could try it out on your grandchildren.
8. Starting a podcast about how shit it is getting old. Older people are far too positive sometimes

> and maybe the balance needs to be shifted. Say things about young people that they say about you and you might go viral and start earning a bit. No, not that type of viral.

My personal solution to loneliness would be to pool resources with friends and live together in a house, so at least you know in advance you would like each other and you're aware of what people's shortcomings are. Mine are many and varied and I would imagine if I reached a certain old age, I'd probably start proper smoking again and possibly drinking too. In fact, I would imagine most of us would, so pissed and pissing with gay abandon. Although it's not a guarantee, you probably stand more chance with a group of people you know.

At some point you may have to contend with you or someone else developing dementia. At least your friends would know you well enough to spot the signs very early on and carry out your wishes. You could make a pact never to play bingo or sing wartime songs, for example. It would be like living in a student house together and you'd probably manage a similar level of incontinence, just for different reasons.

THINGS YOU CAN STOP DOING WHEN YOU'RE OLD

1. Dressing up. I don't mean as Long John Silver or Margaret Thatcher, but tarting yourself up for endurance tests disguised as posh evenings, dinner parties - anything formal, especially where someone tries to pull your chair out for you.
2. Going to activities specifically for old people.
3. Eating healthily, if you were. I wasn't anyway.
4. Wearing your 'just in case I have a road accident' pants out.
5. Not swearing at members of the clergy.
6. Being on time for things. People expect you to be late.
7. Telling the truth. Tell whopping great lies and see if it makes any difference whatsoever.
8. Decanting sauces into more attractive containers.
9. Putting things away tidily. Just sling them into the nearest available hole.
10. Pretending you like presents that are hideous.

CHAPTER NINETEEN

Animal Magic

The animal kingdom has a great deal to teach us about looking after the older members of a group. You might be surprised about which animal we're going to start with. Here's a clue: children are always asking them the time, or they did in my day. Just in case you were thinking, 'Is it chimpanzees who have learned to tell the time?' No, it is of course the wolf, or 'Mr Wolf' to you.

Wolves have not had a good rap over the years, as is evidenced by the murderous, hungry Mr Wolf and numerous familiar bits of anti-wolf propaganda – phrases like 'a wolf in sheep's clothing' and 'keep the wolf from the door' implying that wolves are dangerous and impose themselves on you like scam builders. When we were children, our dad would often say to us that we were 'wolfing' down our food if we were eating too fast, which was normally the case at every meal. And let's not forget the familiar trope of wolves 'howling at the moon' in those oh-so-common shots beloved of old-fashioned horror films. Incidentally, the howling has absolutely nothing to do with the moon. Wolves point their noses towards the sky so their howl, which serves to round up their pack, will carry further. Don't say I don't ever teach you anything.

I think it's time wolves are given the respect they deserve. I reckon the oft-maligned old wolf must be livid with creatures like the much-loved robin. Adorning most Christmas cards and looking cute in gardens, whilst secretly most robins are concealing a *terrible* reputation. For example, robins will fatally wound other robins to protect their food source. Even I wouldn't go that far. And they fight each other for territory all the time.

So, let's look at how wolves deserve a bit more understanding instead of always being seen as the villains of the animal world. Firstly, wolves do cooperative hunting in packs and share their food with the whole family. I didn't really share stuff with my brothers, although at least I was not the child in my family who saved their sweets until my oldest brother and I had eaten ours, and then mercilessly flaunted them in front of us, resulting in mild robin-like behaviour in return. Wolves also share their food with injured and older members of the pack, who can no longer hunt efficiently. So, when I'm no longer able to stalk my prey in the aisles at Sainsbury's, I may well join a wolf pack. Wolves will also surround weaker, older wolves to protect them from other predators, and they will groom and care for the older wolves who can't look after themselves. I must admit I'm warming to wolves and I'm pretty sure I'm going to need a fair bit of grooming when I'm ancient. In fact, I could do with it now. I do hope I have rehabilitated Mr Wolf and his mates, and enabled people to see that Grandma Wolf is a very lucky female.

Here are some other honourable mentions of responsible members of the animal kingdom. Let's start with lions, who have been observed to guide older lions to the softer bits of a dead buffalo. Yes, don't think about it too much. I'm sure the England Lionesses give the same preference to the older players when their buffalo wings are delivered. And African wild dogs go hunting to provide food for the older dogs as well as the pups. Sounds like sending someone out for a takeaway, doesn't it? They haven't progressed to Elephant Deliveroo yet, but I'm sure it's only a matter of time. But I would imagine that if elephants ever do get the chance to request what they want to eat, they'd be very pissed off if Elephant Deliveroo gets it even slightly wrong, because an elephant never forgets.

I have always found elephants very charming. They do indeed have remarkable long-term memory, allowing them to remember water sources for years, safe havens, food and the fiver you lent them in 2023. (On the other hand, if I lent you a fiver last night, I've already forgotten about it.) But the main reason is because they care for both older and very young members of the herd. Their deep social bonds mean that younger elephants support older ones by helping them walk and find food, but they also protect them from threats. And this happens particularly as the older elephants' teeth fail and their mobility decreases. Younger members of the herd will also adapt diets for some older elephants and ensure they have easily digestible food, and they will find soft ground for the older elephants. Who knew? They seem to have a lot of skills. I'm starting to think they would be wonderful in any care setting. Dumbo: not so very dumb any more, is he?

In return, the older females provide crucial leadership and knowledge, and they show empathy through physical touch and coordinated group care. 'Older females'? 'Crucial leadership'? You don't see those words next to each other in a sentence often enough in my view – big up the elephants.

Other noble qualities about which elephants can boast are that they can recognize themselves in the mirror (which is not something I can say after a particularly gruelling sesh in a make-up chair), they use tools to the extent they employ small branches held in their trunks to scratch their backs (we've all been there) and, if they're available, termite mounds and safari vehicles to rub themselves against (haven't tried this). Must be slightly terrifying if you're the person in the vehicle at the time.

They also attempt on occasion to help other species

too, having been witnessed trying to rescue dogs and even a baby rhino stuck in mud.

It is reassuring to know there are some caring wild animals, and it is from this group that humans first started to domesticate them as pets. Sadly, I'm not talking about elephants here. Imagine trying to take one to the vet. The first time pets were kept by humans was in Egypt and Asia, and people obviously thought they were great to be around, so wolves were tamed and gradually morphed into dogs. They started off as guard dogs, herders and hunters. So, think sheepdogs, Alsatians and any dogs that are good at hunting, which probably covers most of them apart from some tiny little yappy things and any dog with very short legs, who can probably only hunt snails.

Cats appeared first in Cyprus, where human skeletons have been discovered buried alongside them. Don't think I'll be adding that to my funeral plan.

When I was a child, lots of people seemed to have birds in cages, which is now hugely frowned upon and has gradually become quite rare. Birds in cages must be registered nowadays, and it's always seemed a bit cruel to me to contain them in this way, although I could have done with some big cages when the kids were little, to keep them safe while I did the housework in three and a half minutes. My grandma and grandad had a parrot called Gussie, who seemed quite chirpy. I always thought Gussie's vocabulary was quite limited, and in those days I was a charming little girl, so I did not teach him any rude words. Although he did keep saying, 'Who's a pretty boy then?' Unfortunately, no one ever answered him, so he never really knew that he was.

Since my parents died, I now have their diaries and one of my dad's entries detailed finding a budgie in a wardrobe and being unable to ascertain what it was doing there, as no one in the house owned a budgie! This odd little story was followed by the news that I had been born. Second billing to a budgie, eh?

A lot of older people do like to have a non-human companion (a pet, not a robot) to keep them company. This could either be because no one else likes them any more, or they failed to keep up Christmas card ping-pong and lost touch with friends. Or maybe they just prefer animals to humans. There are plenty of people like that around. (Incidentally, there is only one thing worse than no Christmas cards and that's cards with reams and reams of turgid 'family news' about Toby managing to put on his own socks, Graham finishing *The Times* crossword or Grandad having a prostate operation. Enough of my Christmas cheer.)

Pets, mainly cats and dogs in this country, do change the atmosphere in your house if you're living on your own, by giving it a feeling of homeliness, by stretching out in front of the fire, sleeping on your bed and barking when the postman or scammers knock on the door. Dogs require quite a lot of input, whereas cats come and go as they please providing you feed them. A friend of mine whose cat regularly disappeared for long periods put a message on its collar asking people to call her if they were feeding it. She got *nine* calls.

However, you can never guarantee with cats whether they're even going to like you much. Sod's law decrees that the ones that particularly don't like you are the fluffy, cute-looking ones. At one point we had several cats and kittens. One cat got so fed up with being bullied by her brother she moved next door. We see her most days and she never looks the least bit inclined to come back. Dogs, however, love anyone that feeds them. That's not a bad basis for a relationship.

The huge problem for cat and dog owners more recently is vet's bills, which, since conglomerates have taken over surgeries, have rocketed, with prices not so much steadily rising as zooming way beyond the reach of most people. Luckily, quite a lot of charities will take up the slack, and as most of you probably know, animal welfare charities do a lot better for donations compared to human ones.

Unfortunately, if you're an elderly person, and it is normally women who tend to acquire multiple cats, often there comes a time when you simply can't cope and you become that cliché, 'a crazy cat lady'. I can't say I've ever heard the equivalent, 'a crazy cat man', although if you put a comma in between the last two words, you will discover a phrase many hippies used to say about the more experimental drug user in their group of friends.

Neither cats nor dogs can look after you, unfortunately. Our dog has never brought me a cup of tea once. Although dogs alerting people to the fact that someone is ill or in danger is a common phenomenon. There are designated 'medical assistance' dogs who can alert owners about undetectable changes in their smell which may presage illnesses such as cancer, diabetes and bacterial infections, or just that they're not showering enough. And I must give an honourable mention to dogs who are trained to give comfort to older people with dementia and reduce their anxiety. They are the all-round good guys of the animal world for older people. And of course, since guide dogs came into being in the early 1930s in this country because of the huge numbers of soldiers blinded in the First World War, the range of assistance dogs has expanded beyond recognition. Dogs are loyal and kind creatures, unless they are treated badly, so of course they're a safe bet as carers.

So, what does the future hold for older people who want to sit by the fire with a cat on their lap? I have a vision of one of those realistic pet toys for children, handily programmed not to eat or poo, which sorts out some of the issues that may be a problem with real pets. (Robot cat, anyone?) They could also be programmed to fetch medication, miaow when it must be taken and go to the shops for teabags. Almost like a little fluffy human. I've always wanted to use the word 'anthropomorphize' in a sentence and here it is.

I think there are quite a lot of elderly people who would like to leave all their money to their pets in their wills, so if that is you, bear in mind that for the purpose of inheritance, pets are treated as property rather than living things deserving of a solid gold drinking bowl or a trip round the mice haunts of your neighbourhood. This is why many people leave everything to animal charities, rather than their named pet.

Apparently, quite a few care homes are happy for you to bring your pet to live in the place with you. Imagine that! Wouldn't they make an absolutely marvellous addition to your experience in a different and very unfamiliar place? I might get a pet rat as a surprise just to put the wind up Matron.

Of course, the older people living at home with a bit of dosh and the urge to travel will be able to go on a trip to watch our final champion carer of the elderly in the wild. No, it's not a jellyfish, but that leviathan of the deep, the whale. All right, I admit I'm talking about the killer whale, but try not to hold that against them. Older females are the leaders of killer whale pods, which can be anything between five and thirty whales. Both males and females remain with the mother's pod for their entire lives, which allows Grandma Killer Whale, who can live up to the age of 80, to look after her grandchildren and help her daughter become a good mum. So not really part of the sandwich generation then, and I wouldn't advise you to go swimming with orcas, because let's face it, you're going to be the sandwich.

CHAPTER TWENTY

A Technologically Illiterate, Curmudgeonly Old Witch

Do you know anyone who actually *likes* the process of ageing? I can't think of anyone at all, but I can think of a lot of people who actively dislike it or even hate it. Well, you could spend your entire old age being resentful, but what is the point of that unless you enjoy it? I think one way of feeling much more positively about the whole situation is seeing it as an opportunity to think about the sort of person you really are and how you could do *less* of the things you don't like and *more* of what you do. So, here's the route I'm planning on heading down and it will most likely involve the following:

Embracing the invisible life!

I saw a post on a social media platform recently that asked the question, 'Do older women realize that no one likes them or finds them attractive?' Although this was probably written to be provocative or funny, by a humourless numpty who looks like a recently disinterred potato, this old woman will attempt to answer it. Here goes . . .

Don't care. Piss off.

As we know so well, there are many men who seem to feel it is important to make some sort of comment as they walk or drive past a woman on the street to inform her of her suitability as a sexual partner, positively or negatively. Women are used to this and none of them like it apart from maybe about three women. Fielding unwanted comments is something all women are familiar with, and sadly school-age girls too.

I should say that men are not allowed to call out this banal crap to women any more – it's now officially a crime, though it's depressingly still a very common issue. Who actually cheers up when they're walking past a building site? No one, apart from maybe my dad, who loved a bit of scaffolding. I was treated to a volley of abuse from two guys in a white van (you don't say), who referred to my weight and sexual proclivities (wrong on the second count). Unfortunately for them, I must have been in a bad mood, and they were stuck in a traffic jam. I shan't say any more on the subject except that it's amazing how quickly people like me can move when we need to!

One of the many benefits of getting older is that most of the catcalling stops if you're lucky. (Why is it called that? No one's ever asked me if I want some milk . . .) People on building sites don't really care if an old woman is miserable. And, ironically, they haven't worked out that most women look miserable *because* they're walking past a building site. Many women as they age say they feel invisible. To me this is a GOOD THING. However, I realize that is somewhat inappropriate, maybe. I just like being ignored, but I don't think, because you're older, it gives everyone carte blanche to behave as if you're not there.

There is a much-loved chant often heard at Millwall football club, 'No one likes us, we don't care!' I think co-opting that attitude is a good idea as you age, because you know that anyone who is negative or dismissive towards you just because you're older is going to be an arsehole, so bear this in mind. I wouldn't particularly recommend chanting this out loud, though, unless you're very drunk.

Just Saying No

If you don't want to do something, just say no. It's taken me a *long* time to get good at this, because, despite appearances, I am a people-pleaser; lots of women are.

I often hear people-pleasers told that, '*No* is a complete sentence' to help them move on from, 'Er, I'm not sure, I think I've got something on that night, can I get back to you?' That's all very well if you like speaking in extremely short sentences or you are a talented liar. I am neither. There is a compromise somewhere between those two – somewhere along the lines of 'No, I'm sorry I can't do that' usually works. I've not been very good at this myself but am trying to improve.

In my life, I have done a lot of things that I didn't really want to do. I once did a 300-mile round trip to do a benefit as a favour to a friend, despite having to be back the next morning in London. It didn't go brilliantly, but that happens. On the way home I blew a tyre on the M1 and nearly totalled myself, the car and the other comic I had with me. No good deed ever goes unpunished, as they say.

I feel I need to even this up as I have been responsible for a fair few good deeds being punished on more than one occasion. A kind friend once allowed me to borrow their car as mine was laid up in a garage and I drove to Leicester in it with three other comics to do a show. On the way back we pulled into a service station to get some early breakfast. I drove into the lorry park by accident and before I had a chance to rectify this mistake, a massive French juggernaut had backed into us, bashed the front of the car, puncturing the radiator. We managed to limp home in it, but there was no way my friend could drive it to work the next morning. I think she probably sang the 'no good deed' song quite a few times in between cursing me.

I figure that, now I'm old, people will just assume I've become grumpy and let me (not) get on with it. The problem with agreeing to do things you don't really want to do is that resentment builds up and this is not fair on the people who have asked you. It's not their fault you agreed to do something when you didn't really want to, so either suck it up, or behave like a grown-up and sort it out earlier down the line. I'm afraid I'm finding the latter increasingly difficult, so it is much easier to say no in the first place.

Calling out patronizing people

I will aim to always have a few put-downs ready for when people patronize me. A woman in her seventies once came up to me and said she had used one of my heckle put-downs to a bloke in the street who had been rude to her. I was so delighted.

Although it is a good thing for a comic to come up with a heckle put-down specific to the individual heckle, it's not always possible (and certainly not for my old brain, which is working at a third of the speed), but if you come up with something on the spot, credit to you.

Otherwise generically I think I'll try:

'I may look like a stupid old woman, but what you don't seem to realize is that despite appearances I still have a working brain, and I do not like to be addressed as if I am a child. I am perfectly able to function in society and if I wasn't, I wouldn't be here. Do you think I am some sort of intellectually challenged old fool? Well, let me just run you through some of my achievements to give you a chance to change your mind. I have worked continuously since the age of 17, got a degree, brought up a family, and put up with a series of patronizers not dissimilar to you on endless occasions, so please, if you don't mind, I don't *actually* want to cross the road at this point.'

Them, Them, Them to Me, Me, Me

It's very easy to get into a treadmill-type existence just because you're used to it. I'm not talking about the ones at the gym: I've never been drawn to them. No, I mean, life lays itself out in very familiar patterns for long periods of time because you get into a routine. Now, as you get older and slough off some responsibilities, it's easier to stay on the treadmill in some ways, so try and become more familiar with doing what you like, when you like. I realize it's not that easy for everyone, given we're the sandwich generation or caring for a partner, but if you're buckling under the weight of something like this, try to find some time to set aside for you. It may only be a few minutes, but could be longer if you've said no to something. Stay in bed late, watch a crappy film, ignore the housework . . . [insert your preferences here].

Becoming Pedantry Personified

I will be correcting people's grammar, spelling and pronunciation more often going forward into my later years. It drives me nuts and it annoys them. Double the pleasure.

Becoming a semi-professional pedant has been very enjoyable so far. I find it hilarious how these days everyone has a spellchecker on their device and yet spelling is so much worse. God, it's a good thing I can't experience myself the way other people do, I sound unbearable. I was probably the bane of my daughters' lives when they were younger, but they don't half speak lovely.

Dressing Down

I will also be wearing whatever I like. Most people have two different modes of dressing at least, by which I mean 'at home mooching about' and 'going out'. You can, of course, split 'going out' into subsets – going out 'casual', going out 'necessarily very well groomed' (like a horse) and going out to something that requires a new piece of clothing. Well, mooching is fine, but I absolutely *hate* going out dressed very smartly or for a big occasion. There is something about it that makes me feel like I'm wearing a straitjacket and I become a magnet for various substances to land in very prominent positions on my clothing. Ketchup, mayonnaise, curry, whatever is in the vicinity, comes flying through the air and attaches itself to me. I find awards of any kind absolutely excruciating and often find myself guilty of thinking, 'I hope I don't win, because I look terrible, there will be "paps" and I have no clue how to dress myself like a proper lady.' Only once did I ever cast a very wary eye over some social media after an event to see my top garment described as 'billowing' as if I had come to a fancy-dress event as the lead galleon of the Spanish Armada (look it up, kids). It's so stressful, it's hardly worth going, so I don't, and haven't ventured to a big event like that since.

Training to Become a Witch

Many older people and a number in the entertainment business seem to want to keep on working well after retirement age and I can totally understand that. One's sense of self-esteem, being useful to society or, pragmatically speaking, having something to do, can all be thrown into the mix, not to mention just having human company, which is why so many people volunteer for charities.

I haven't explored the possibilities yet, but something I'm thinking of doing is looking into how to become/train as a witch. (Let's face it, I don't look far off one already.) Are you thinking I've gone completely mad? Hope so. There is a tiny bit of method in my madness, but not much, to be honest.

It's simply because I have always felt that I have some sort of indefinable intuitive ability, which I've always wanted to find out more about. Obviously the sceptics among you (and I am normally one) will be shaking your heads or closing this book and I don't blame you. But if you haven't, I will give a few examples. You might have heard them before as I do trot them out from time to time.

Some years ago, I did the show *Taskmaster* and took part in a challenge in which the Taskmaster, Greg Davies, called upon us contestants to predict one of two pictures he was going to show us which were concealed behind a screen, and these two pictures were of a horse or a laminator. (Yes, I don't know either.) Anyway, to cut to the chase, I got thirteen in a row, the odds on that being approximately 8,000 to 1. I have no idea how that happened, but I do know that at one point, all the contestants got up to try to distract me, and after getting one more correct, I felt some sort of shift in my mind occur and got the next one wrong.

'So what?' you might say. 'Is that your evidence for your "intuitive ability"?' Well, the other thing to throw into the mix is that I have had many uncanny coincidences, as we all have, I know. Particularly with one of my daughters. She is always messaging me as I'm messaging her, I often bump into her in weird places, and on numerous occasions I have often been thinking about her when she calls me. I know, it happens to all of us. I wasn't promising that I can turn people into frogs or make milk go off, it just sounds a bit more of an interesting thing to do than gardening. And I won't have to get a new wardrobe.

The main problem with giving advice on how to approach getting older is that it is inevitably 'one size fits all' and every single older person is different, so the only person who can decide whether you want to do certain things is you. But perhaps there is some fun and freedom to be found in old stereotypes. Perhaps if we have a look at some of the clichés abounding about types of old people then you could create a game with your family or do a secret ballot so you can see which of the stereotypes they think you fall into. Obviously, I am an 'old witch', as discussed, but I suspect I am a mix of 'technologically illiterate' and 'curmudgeon' too. (I rather like the alternative term for women – 'termagant'. I can tell people I am one and then make up the definition myself as no one will have even heard of it.) I do strongly recommend finding an 'old person' stereotype and leaning into it, just for the hell of it. There is some real fun to be had, and you may want to operate on a pick 'n' mix basis and take a little from all of them.

Not an exhaustive list by any means, but ones that spring to mind are:

THE CURMUDGEON: mainly applied to men being grumpy. The sort of bloke who chases you down the road waving a stick at you and shouting, 'Get off my land!' When we lived in a sleepy Kent village my dad used to chase away 'yobs' hanging round the war memorial outside our house and was known as 'Old Man Brand' at the ripe old age of 35. But there is no reason this shouldn't be an equal opportunities category!

THE DOTING GRANDPARENT: the sort who gives sweets and then eats most of them to protect the teeth of the recipients.

THE YOUNG AT HEART: often found in night-clubs inappropriately dressed and off their faces.

THE TECHNOLOGICALLY ILLITERATE: the ones who point at their phones/computers and say, 'What does this mean?' a lot.

THE WISE: in my family it was my grandad who always knew which horse was going to win the 3.30 at Doncaster. Except he often didn't.

THE WELL-PRESERVED: usually applied to women. Makes them sound like a jar of pickled onions or a museum exhibit and I know what I'd rather have in my fridge.

THE APPLE-CHEEKED: again, usually women who tend to exist in books like *The Darling Buds of May* or children's books about farms.

THE MOANING MISERY: yep, I'm definitely partly in this camp.

THE CBA or THE CAN'T BE ARSED: this is very much my area of expertise. The CBAs leave it longer and longer between trips to the hairdressers or barbers, wear no make-up, or let their nose and ear hair get too long, and sport any old sack that comes to hand.

So, once you've decided which one of these you are, enjoy them. Much as I'd like to be an apple-cheeked, well-preserved, wise, young at heart type of old woman, I fear none of these are within my reach. Still, I think there is huge enjoyment to be had with all of the others, so good luck with them and happy ageing (apart from the well-preserved, obviously).

THINGS AGE HAS MADE ME MORE INTOLERANT OF

1. Carol singers who can't sing. Give them a klaxon blast after three seconds if necessary, or tell them you have called the police.
2. People in the cinema/theatre who won't stop talking/texting/eating/sleeping/coughing/sniffing/snoring/rustling/fidgeting/scratching/humming/singing/trying to find their phone in their bag/looking for a sweet they've dropped etc., etc., etc.
3. Old people.
4. Drivers who lean on their horn behind you because you haven't moved off 0.003 of a second after the lights changed. Time to stall the engine.
5. Children who expect you to get out of their way. Just walk straight at them. They've got more energy to walk round you than you have to circumnavigate them.

THINGS I'VE MELLOWED ON

1. Products being in different places in a supermarket when you go back a week later. I just buy whatever's there now.
2. People who like courgettes, but I've only mellowed a tiny bit. People who expect me to eat them: no change.
3. Old people.
4. Dogs with outfits and shoes on.
5. Road signs that are so dirty you can't read them. I just drive home. Bonus!

CHAPTER TWENTY ONE

Last Word

Well, my brain feels slightly emptier after that. I hope you got something out of it . . . even a few hollow laughs and some tutting would do me.

I suppose if you felt like it – and I think it's a good idea for a lot of us – you could have a go at writing some sort of book or diary yourself. I'm saying this because I have derived so much pleasure and interest from reading my mum and dad's self-published books. The word 'vanity' is often attached to this sort of publishing, but whether it's vain or not is neither here nor there to me. My dad's book is autobiographical, contains lots of things I didn't know and is a hoot. My mum's book is a collection of her favourite sayings, quotes and poems, so very different from my dad's, but equally fascinating.

The letters written between my mum and dad before

they got married are also precious to me. He was stationed at various army bases in the UK, having to do his national service before being posted to Libya, and his letters are mainly geographical in their detail. My mum's by contrast very domesticated. Who knew that just before my mum got married, she was doing cookery classes? I just *cannot* imagine it, given the sort of woman she became as she morphed over the years into a divorced and somewhat bolshy feminist. I realize a lot of you will think I'm ancient suggesting a book or a diary, but what else will there be in generations to come to tell your offspring about you? Someone's Instagram page or their TikTok posts will hardly cover all the bases and may well be lost in the ether!

I'm sure my children are *really* looking forward to receiving their own personal copy of this book. Should I sign it to them individually, I wonder, as this might mean they can't offload it quite so easily at a charity shop? Hmm, something to ponder. Although I'm hoping they'll enjoy it, by the time they get round to it, reading might not be a thing anymore and some new bit of kit will have been developed on audiobooks, so they'll be able to absorb it while they're asleep or swallow it as a tablet. Not the portable computer thingy, she said, in rather complex technical language.

If *you* didn't like this book much, you could always pass it on as a revenge present to someone who got you a really crappy present last year. If you're a similar age to me, not far off 70, I hope you got something out of my efforts. I realize that everyone's attitude towards ageing is very different, but I'd hope you might want to ask yourself some questions. And perhaps it's good to ask yourself these questions a bit earlier than you need to . . .

Are you happy just to be carried along by the tide of however ageing affects you?

How do you want things to be if you can't cope at home?

Are you happy for your family, near or far, to leave you marinading in your clutter until you can't be seen behind the debris, or do you want them to come round, have a good old clear-out and send you off to be looked after?

Who, of all the people you know, had a good old age and how did they do it? From what I hear of my great-grandmother, she just went to bed and ate chocolate all day. Bring it on!

Should you give your family some instructions or requests? I don't mean, 'Please could you move me into Buckingham Palace,' or 'Please get me a chauffeur'. Probably easier to say what you don't want. Do your kids want to look after you? Or do they want *you* to look after *their* children? Or have they gone to Australia? Or can't you stand them? All these sorts of issues may influence your decisions as Old Father/Mother/Parent Time speeds up to a brisk trot.

Or maybe just stick your head in the sand until it's too late, which is probably what I'll end up doing.

There are many ways of doing this and I'll always favour the one with the least effort. Personally, I've always favoured sticking my head above the parapet, but I suppose it might be preferable to keep my head down for a change.

My absolute favourite phrase involving sticking your head somewhere is an American playground taunt, 'na-na na-na boo-boo stick your head in doo doo'. Of course, it didn't originally mean what we mean by 'nana,' but I love to commandeer a phrase.

In the end, it's all down to individual preference and timing. So, if you do manage to unfreeze your upper lip, let everyone know your preferences. If you don't, never mind, you've got most of us in your camp with you.

So, here's wishing you the old age you want for yourself and many more Happy Birthdays.

Acknowledgements

Thanks very much to Emma Henderson. Very much enjoyed the café meet-ups and the text message/voice note jousting, Emma! (I expect you can guess who did which.) And thank you to everyone at Penguin: Gaby Young, Kara Nielson, Mubarak Elmubarak and Bea McIntyre.

And as ever huge thanks to Vivienne Clore, my agent and friend, who read the book and whose judgement I rate extremely highly.

And a general thanks to everyone who helped or didn't hinder me. As the possessor of an extremely patchy memory even before I started to get older, I'm sure you know who you are.

And thanks, family, as always.

And finally, to all the people I loved to bits who aren't here anymore. I miss you all very much.